A WOMAN'S INNER WORLD

Selected Poetry and Prose of Anne Bradstreet

Edited with an Introduction by

Adelaide P. Amore

UNIVERSITY
PRESS OF
AMERICA

Library of Congress Catalog Card Number: **82-40198**

As weary pilgrim, now at rest,
Hugs with delight his silent, nest
His wasted limbes, now lye full soft
That myrie steps, have troden oft
Blesses himself, to think upon
his dangers past and travailes done
The burning sun no more shall heat
Nor stormy raines, on him shal beat
The bryars and thornes no more shall scratch
nor hungry wolves at him shall catch
He erring pathes no more shall treed
Nor wild fruits eate, in stead of bread
for waters cold he doth not long
for thirst no more shall parch his tongue
No rugged stones his feet shall gaule
nor stumps nor rocks cause him to fall
All cares and feares he bids farwell
and meanes in safity now to dwel
A pilgrim I on earth perplext
wth sinns wth cares and sorrows vext
by age and paines brought to decay
and my Clay house mouldring away
how I long to be at rest
soare on high among the blest

To Arnold, Arnie, Aaron, and Thor who understand the importance of a woman's inner world.

ACKNOWLEDGEMENTS

I wish to express my special thanks to a number of individuals whose encouragement and expertise served to help me complete this book: Professor Louis Martz, English Department, Yale University, who kindly provided me with assistance in making editing decisions; Professor Joan McCarthy, English Department, Southern Connecticut, who gave constructive suggestions throughout this project; Reference Librarian Susan Searing of the Sterling Memorial Library, Yale University, whose comments and suggestions for this bibliography were valuable; to my sister Anne whose support and kindness aided me in the final preparation of this manuscript.

For permission to reproduce the M S poem entitled "A Weary Pilgrim," I am indebted to the Stevens Memorial Library, North Andover, Massachusetts, owner of the Bradstreet Manuscript and to its former trustee, Buchanan Charles, who brought the M S back home. Mr. Russell Reeve, Director of the Stevens Memorial Library, deserves thanks for his gracious help on resources and production matters.

Adelaide P. Amore
Department of English
Southern Connecticut
State College
New Haven, Connecticut

April 1982

TABLE OF CONTENTS

Page

I.

We stand in a fine gallery admiring the portraits of
two distinguished seventeenth century American
statesmen. Between the two portraits is a carefully
measured space designed for a third work, but its
space holds only a carefully centered gold
inscription plate. We move closer and discover the
plate bears a woman's name; we realize she bears a
relationship to the two men, but our curiousity,
peaked by the missing portrait, sends us to a library
in search of the mysterious woman's true identity.

At the library, we learn the woman's occupation:
poet. To view her early editions, now prized, we
require a curator's special permission. Not everyone
may touch the small, aging, leather-bound volumes:
the first and second editions of her works. We
search carefully through each volume for the woman's
portrait, but we find none. We note the short,
simple poems and meditations, and the long,
historical works, but still we wish to see her face.
We notice the poet's brother-in-law, John Woodbridge,
provided a careful introduction for the first
edition, but it takes precedence over the poet's own
prologue. We look on. There must be a portrait in
one of the editions. We search through the
eighteenth and nineteenth century editions;

surprisingly, we find the same familiar portraits of
the poet's husband and father adorning the
traditional place of the artist's. What a strange
and curious predicament! The poet's relatives are
memorialized, but not the poet. Finally, we find a
sketch of a Puritan woman in one edition. This must
be the missing figure, we initially think. Checking
other historical sources, we learn the picture is not
one of the poet; in fact, it is not even authentic
for the poet's period.

Undeterred, we continue our search. We find a
picture of the poet's home in another edition. Here
then at Andover, Massachusetts, in the intimate
surroundings of the poet's daily life, the answer is
to be found. We search and discover the picture has
mistakenly been designated as that of her home.
Another historical fraud, now corrected, steals our
hope.

In dismay, we turn to biographies. Perhaps those
careful historical scholars will paint the poet's
portrait for us. A biography of this unique poet
measured by male biographies of the seventeenth
century promises us a work filled with rich, fine
detail; yet, the opposite proves true. The details
of her life are curiously and painfully incomplete.
Her birthdate is often marked by 1612? at
Northampton, England; her comely face, we are told,
is nowhere to be found; no portraits or drawings
exist. In her home, we learn this woman received
love and respect as a wife and mother; outside her
home, honors came in terms of her connections to the
male members of her family. The greatest compliment
she received was that she was worthy of her father
and husband; thus, even as we examine the letters and
historical documents of the period, our poet's
identity remains unclear. Critics refer to her as a
"pleasing figure. . .who was 'fathered and husbanded'
respectively by Thomas Dudley and Simon Bradstreet,
both in their time governors of Massachusetts."[1]

---

[1]William P. Trent et. al. Cambridge History of
American Literature (New York: Putnam, 1917), I,
154.

Even in death, these two distinguished men dominate the poet's tiny volumes as their portraits replace hers in each frontispiece. In creating the poet's critical portrait, critics consistently characterize her work with terms of apology, condescension, and sexism: "A Right Du Bartas Girlie,"[2] and a person who maintained her "sexual station."[3] But such negative criticism did not deter the poet. Through a lifetime in which she suffered intermittent illnesses, long separations from her husband, eight difficult childbirths, and the deaths of her beloved grandchildren and daughter-in-law, she created her art. In the midst of the everyday crises of early New England living, she stole a few precious moments to compose her verses, contemplations, and meditations in spite of the belief that writing poetry was a frivolous activity for a woman.[4]

In a world where as many as half the women could only sign by a mark, she read the classical and popular poets of her day, understood and applied the Bible's teachings to her practical existence, and wrote with clarity, purpose, and, occasionally, humor. In a society that thought a woman's education consisted mainly of "training of how to conduct and care for the home,"[5] this woman lived as avid student, devoted wife, loving mother, and gifted artist.

Our search goes on. In the detailed accounts of her family's life, the historical records of the Massachusetts Bay Colony, the early governors, Dudley and Bradstreet, and inevitably, the poet's work, we find parts of her true identity. We proceed through

---

[2]Nathaniel Ward, "Untitled Verse about the Authoresse," Tenth Muse (London: Bowtell, 1650), 5.

[3]The Founding of a Nation, ed. Kenneth Silverman (New York: Collier-McMillan, 1971), 13.

[4]Josephine Piercy, The Tenth Muse (Grainsville, Florida: Scholars' Facsimiles, 1965), x.

[5]Carl Halliday, Woman's Life in Colonial Days (Williamstown, Mass.: Corner House, 1968), 94.

xiii

the painstaking examination of each tiny and complicated fragment; we piece together the poet's life. This then is the composite of a woman's inner world, the portrait of America's first published poet: The Tenth Muse, Anne Bradstreet.

II.

Anne Bradstreet's life began happily as a privileged one. Born the daughter of Thomas and Dorothy Yorke Dudley near the beginning of the seventeenth century, she lived elegantly at the Earl of Lincoln's estate at Sempringham where her father managed properties. As the favorite of six children, Anne received a fine education from as many as eight tutors.[6] A precocious child, she spent many happy hours reading in the Earl's extensive library, enjoying the beautiful English gardens, and living in comfortably furnished estate rooms.[7]

In the world of English letters, Shakespeare, Marlowe, and Spenser were popular figures, but two writers more in keeping with Anne's literary and philosophical tastes were Sir Walter Raleigh and Guillarme Du Bartas. These choices indicated her independent thinking. Raleigh, considered by his contemporaries a skeptical poet, and Du Bartas, considered by his critics a Calvinist poet, were her favorite writers. In this world of civility, she found solace. In her later life, she recalled two physical crises that interrupted her "scholar's thirst for knowledge... and [her] poet's sensitiveness,"[8] thereby influencing her personal

---

[6] Elizabeth Wade White, "Childhood and Education," in Anne Bradstreet, The Tenth Muse (New York: Oxford University Press, 1971), 42-72.

[7] Josephine Piercy, Anne Bradstreet (New Haven: College and University Press, 1965), 18-19.

[8] Anne Bradstreet, "To My Dear Children," Andover Manuscript, 43-44.

xiv

development: one came when she was six or seven; the Lord sent, she believed, a childhood illness to remind her of obedience and truthfulness; the second occurred when she was fourteen or fifteen; at this point, she reported, her heart "grew more carnal." Were these the signs of her awakening sexuality? Anne's reference to this period is brief, but we do know her long and tender relationship with the young man who was soon to be her husband, Simon Bradstreet, was already in existence. But these first experiences with illness and passion became important elements in the poet's work and reappeared as the "vanities and follies of youth."[9]

In 1628, the childhood sweethearts, Anne Dudley, sixteen, and Simon Bradstreet, twenty-five, married, and, if, as some critics suggest, her father arranged the marriage, it was one both partners welcomed, and as fate would have it, Simon Bradstreet's political and economic life entwined with that of his father-in-law, Thomas Dudley. Anne had little idea the regular meetings her husband and father attended held the foundations of the family's future within them. In less than two short years, plans for the Massachusetts Bay Colony Company brought Dudley, Bradstreet, and other prominent men such as John Winthrop into a tightly knit group. Protecting strict Puritan values from such leaders as Bishop Laud and establishing their own economic independence in a new land became powerful goals among these men. With the final decision to move to the new wilderness, the Dudley and Bradstreet family futures changed dramatically. Anne, over-shadowed by her beloved male associates, lost her identity as an individual and became defined only by her role as woman: "Thomas Dudley, whose daughter afterward became the wife of Governor Bradstreet."[10]

_____

[9]Bradstreet, "To My Dear Children."

[10]Charles M. Andrews, The Colonial Period of American History (New Haven: Yale University Press, 1934), 384.

xv

Thus love and obedience sealed Anne's fate. On March 29, 1630, the Dudleys and Bradstreets boarded the Arbella, one of eleven ships destined to establish the City of God in the wilderness of North America, and set sail. After a difficult and stormy voyage, the Arbella arrived in Salem on June 12, 1630, and a new chapter in American life began.[11] The men of the Massachusetts Bay Colony were unique settlers. They were well educated (Oxford, Trinity, and Cambridge), dogmatic in matters of religion, and astute in matters of politics.[12] They ruled the churches, governments, and social communities with their newly incorporated power and built their City of God without intervention from the British crown. This new society placed God at the center of all its thought and banned all "drama, sacred music, and erotic poetry."[13] This society regarded men as superior to women and one male leader went so far as to proclaim that a woman should "derive her ideas of God from the contemplations of her husband's excellencies."[14]

There is no doubt Anne Bradstreet admired her husband and father; her poems are filled with their praises, but we wonder if the oppression of female initiative and expression, or perhaps the untimely death of Lady Arbella, a friend and shipmate of Anne's, inspired or provoked her phrase, "my heart rose," and later, "[I] submitted to it and joined the church at Boston,"[15]

---

[11]Andrews, 395.

[12]Franklin Bowditch Dexter, A Selection From Miscellaneous Papers of Fifty Years (New Haven: Tuttle, Morehouse and Taylor, 1918), 102-105.

[13]Samuel Morison, The Intellectual Life of Colonian New England (New York: New York University Press, 1956), 12.

[14]Andrews, 477.

[15]Bradstreet, "To My Dear Children." 45.

rather than the frequent critical notion that it was prompted by her revulsion at the primitiveness of the new world. Within the confines of her well-to-do family, Anne found the protection and attention of two loving, influential men, but any woman who sought to use her wit, charm, or intelligence in the community at large found herself ridiculed, banished, or executed by the Colony's powerful group of male leaders. The affairs of church and state were clearly within the male domain, while women managed the domestic ones.

There were, even in those early, difficult days of the Colony's founding, women who chose to enter the mainstream of Puritan religious life. Anne Hutchinson was a classic example. Like her contemporary Anne Bradstreet, she came from a prosperous family who recognized her vigorous intellect and provided her with tutorial instruction.[16] Both young women were deeply religious, but Anne Hutchinson turned her attention to ministering to the sick and engaging in religious polemics, while Anne Bradstreet initially began writing imitative verses praising her heroes: Sir Walter Raleigh, Plutarch, Usher, and Du Bartas. Both women were prolific mothers: Hutchinson bore fourteen children; Bradstreet eight. While Bradstreet read her poetic creations at private family gatherings, Hutchinson, a dynamic speaker, chose the open forum. At Thursday afternoon prayer sessions, Hutchinson immediately gained a following of women who were attracted to her charm, while the clergy, especially John Cotton, a preacher Hutchinson followed to the new world, initially supported her religious and ethical debating.[17] Ironically, it was the same John Cotton who preached at Anne

---

[16] Charles and Mary Beard, Growth of Social and Intellectual Autonomy (New York: Doubleday, 1940), 60.

[17] Thomas Hutchinson, The History of Massachusetts Bay Colony (Boston: Printed by Thomas and John Fleet, 1769), Chapter 1.

Bradstreet's English parish, St. Botolph's, while he served as Hutchinson's religious mentor. But Hutchinson's popularity was short lived, for in a society that perceived women as intellectual inferiors such independence was intolerable. Even as highly respected a man as Governor John Winthrop believed women could not bear intellectual rigor without irreparable harm.

> Mr. Hopkins, the governor of Hartford upon Connecticut, came to Boston, and brought his wife with him, (a godly young woman, and of special parts), who was fallen into a sad infirmity, the loss of her understanding and reason, which had been growing upon her divers years, by occasion of her giving herself wholly to reading and writing, and had written many books. Her husband, being very loving and tender of her, was loath to grieve her; but he saw his error, when it was too late. For if she had attended her household affairs, and such things as belong to women, and not gone out of her way and calling to meddle in such things as are proper for men, whose minds are stronger, etc., she had kept her wits, and might have improved them usefully and honorably in the place God had set her. He brought her to Boston, and left her with her brother, one Mr. Yale, a merchant, to try what means might he had here for her. But no help could be had.[18]

In the light of such beliefs, it was no surprise Hutchinson's open expression eventually caused male consternation. One of her views was particularly threatening to the male church officials. She stated the "Holy Ghost dwells personally in a

---

[18]John Winthrop, _Winthrop's Journal: The History of New England_, ed. James K. Hosmer (New York: Charles Scribner's, 1908), II, 225.

justified person," but that justification was not contingent upon the clergy's acknowledging any series of good works necessary for admission to its church. A court of forty men including Thomas Dudley and John Winthrop sat in judgement of the now frail, forty-five year old woman who defended herself. Hutchinson argued eloquently and rationally. She demanded those who charged her be sworn in and give their testimony. This request denied, the court continued its religious debate. When Hutchinson said what she spoke came to her by "immediate revelation" and her attackers would be punished, she found herself under merciless attack and immediate judgement.

Condemned to banishment, Hutchinson asked the reason. Governor Winthrop answered; "Say no more, the court knows wherefore, and is satisfied." Dudley thought her "deluded by the devil," and John Cotton abandoned her.[19] Banished, she lived in Rhode Island and later in New York; there, the woman labelled the American Jezebel met her untimely death, the victim of an unprovoked Indian attack. This brutal slaying reinforced God's approval of the banishment decision, and Winthrop wrote without passion of sympathy: "They [Indians] came to Mrs. Hutchinson's in way of friendly neighborhood, as they had been accustomed, and taking their opportunity killed her. . . .[20]

As a result of Hutchinson's banishment and that of Roger Williams and other dissidents, the Church of Boston reaffirmed its tight community control. For the individual who did not hold firmly to the Church's view that good works and proper religious behavior were the only means of acceptance into membership, the Church adopted extraordinary penalties. How strange that Hutchinson's initial female prayer meetings designed so women could discuss Scriptures should ultimately serve as the

---

[19]Hutchinson, Chapter 1.

[20]Winthrop, II, 138.

source of her social castigation. While men met regularly, women were excluded from their meetings; but soon, the men, impressed by reports of the women's meetings, began attending them while still denying women access to the segregated male religious discussions. For an individual parent, the Church withheld or denied baptism for children or the promise of eternal salvation where compliance was not forthcoming, but Hutchinson's case had even more far reaching consequences. "The spiritual and secular power of the Puritan church curbed active feminine leadership for a hundred years."[21] Hutchinson's trial and the general reprisal system were likely subjects for conversation in the Bradstreet and Dudley homes as politics and religion constituted essential parts of both families' lives and livelihoods. Caldwell suggests the twenty year delay in the publication of Anne Bradstreet's first edition resulted directly from Hutchinson's purge and the prevailing repressive climate.[22] Thus, what critics report as a lack of interest or determination may, in fact, be a practical response to the realities of her day: a woman had no chance of publishing her work; or, as Miller suggests, she obediently accepted the established views of the Puritan church and its aesthetic ideal, wherein no poet should surrender to "sensual delights" and should comply to a "code of plain style" in both rhythms and prose.[23] These practical and aesthetic standards shed light on the long-delayed publication of even Bradstreet's second edition, and indicate why the poet kept her works of a passionate, personal nature secure in her family papers and marked private. Some of these selections

[21]An Account of Anne Bradstreet, The Puritan Poet and Kindred Topics, ed. Colonel Luther Caldwell (Boston: Damrell and Upham, 1898), 29.

[22]Caldwell, 29.

[23]The American Puritans: Their Prose and Poetry, ed. Perry Miller (New York: Doubleday, 1956), 265.

found their way into the second edition, while others did not see publication for another two centuries. Bradstreet clearly set aside her innermost thoughts as a legacy to her children. In her message "To My Dear Children," she confesses her own personal religious doubts and, in other verses, she uses the only socially acceptable device open to women of her time to challenge unfair male views: wit. Even in this, her remarks were dismissed. No one need tell Anne Bradstreet the price women paid for independent, public expression. She was well aware of it.

In dealing with women who sought public audiences, men used two common threats: madness or witchcraft. In a less spectacular but representative case, Margaret Jones, a health healer of sorts, faced indictment for witchcraft. In treating her patients with herbal medicines used as physics and stroking them as a form of therapy, she found disfavor with the authorities. To the seventeenth century male mind, her behaviour caused the "apprehension of physicians and surgeons,"[24] so Jones underwent trial, conviction, and, predictably, hanging.

Historians tell us the intellectual average for the Massachusetts Bay Colony male was high. There were many who had attended Oxford or Cambridge, the latter a Puritan stronghold and Simon Bradstreet's alma mater. For Puritan males, public recognition and material success were signs of God's special favor. Their church supported the view that heaven could be gained by only an elect few--those men who succeeded in their worldly endeavors. The few women, however, who sought to expand their intellectual and creative talents beyond the confines of their homes found themselves in the center of an oppressive atmosphere.[25] As a result, women wondered how they should attain heaven when barred from participating in the process that should help them gain it.

---

[24]Winthrop, II, 344.

[25]Dexter, 102-105.

Prominent clergy such as John Cotton and Cotton Mather had through their pulpits ready-made audiences for their long discourses, but they were eager for even larger ones. Ministers often sent their works to England for printing. Although the final prints had errors and various unpredictable changes in them, such publications did provide recognition for their authors in England and the new world. The same was not true for any woman artist, and particularly for a woman in Anne Bradstreet's social position, such publication appeared impossible.[26]

III.

While we have no evidence to suggest Anne Bradstreet really believed her works might achieve a public audience, we do know she did revise the first edition selections soon after they were published. This suggests an intent to publish the corrected forms along with new pieces that specifically refer to those in the first edition. We know the original selections, presented to her father Thomas, came into the possession of Anne's brother-in-law John Woodbridge who took them to England where he arranged for their printing. In 1650, under the title The Tenth Muse, Lately Sprung Up in America, Bradstreet's work became the first example of new world literature. English readers, always interested in news from the wilderness, eagerly read and approved this effort. At home, the reception seems somewhat mixed. Bradstreet herself reacted strongly to the great number of printing errors she found in the text and began work on a revised edition. Entitled Several Poems, the second edition, published in Boston in 1678, provides much valuable information. First, although we do not know the precise extent of her revisions, we know Bradstreet reviewed, corrected, and added new poems. The Boston edition

---

[26]Morison, The Intellectual Life of Colonial New England, 118.

contains the original "Four Elements," "Four Humours," "Four Ages of Man," "Four Seasons of the Year," "Four Monarchies," and miscellaneous and posthumous poems. Major critics center their remarks around these historical and imitative poems while they pay little attention to those which place emphasis on the inner world of the seventeenth century artist.

In addition, the curious span of time between the first and second editions demands attention. If the poet's revised work was ready, why was there no earlier second edition? One fact that obscures our ability to answer this question is the restrictions that surrounded publication procedures. A woman simply could not arrange for her own work to be printed. Bradstreet did, however, edit first edition selections and write others--far more weighty evidence of her intent; so, the relation of the delay to Bradstreet's desires can not be conjectured. Those critics who see her as a woman with an aversion to artistic recognition must carefully re-examine that position. Twenty-eight years after the first edition appeared, and eight years after the poet's death, the second edition appeared. In 1678, the poet's relative, President John Rogers of Harvard, the individual some believe completed the final editing, published the edition and included his own poem of praise.[27] Rogers' elegy served to spark the creative impulse of one John Norton of Hingham, a clergyman with little knowledge of Anne Bradstreet's work, who wrote of the poet's verses nonetheless. Such a peculiar practice had benefits for those who sought publication credits. Warren reports: "The chief occasion when the arts might be practiced as a pious duty was the death of some friend, relative, or eminent person. Then a funeral elegy was appropriate not only for addition to the memorial stone but, at more ambitious length, for circulation as appended to the biography or printed as a black-boarded

---

[27]Jeannine Hensley, "The Editor of Anne Bradstreet's Several Poems," American Literature, XXXV (1964), 502-505.

broadside."[28] This explains the sudden interest in praising the dead poet; her second edition served to publicize the name of living male writers.

In the "Prologue to the Tenth Muse," the poet's own words speak eloquently of the woman artist's dilemma, but these words, the traditional expression of the poet's purpose, are often overlooked in favor of the detailed accounts of her brother-in-law's introduction to the poet's work, and the previously labelled "humorous" poem by one Nathaniel Ward who chides the poet as imitative and suggests men beware lest women try to wear their (men's) spurs. If we look at the poet's prologue as we should, first, we see she clearly sets the tone for acceptance of her work, and she rightly attempts to establish her audience, just as any other artist might. We know these poems were first given to the poet's father, Thomas Dudley, as a gift. For this reason, critics historically suggest the poet had no aspirations for a larger audience. Her prologue refutes this notion.

I am obnoxious to each carping tongue
Who says my hand a needle better fits
A poet's pen all scorn I should thus wrong
For such despite they [men] cast on female wits,
If what I do prove well, it won't advance,
They'll say it's stol'n, or else it was by chance.

The tone here is obvious. Bradstreet rejects the narrow minded critics who limit her only to passive and stereotyped feminine activities of the home such as needlework. She assesses her poetic efforts realistically, for she knows men consider women intellectually inferior. What greater truth can she utter than the fact she knows her efforts as a woman artist appear as stolen or accidental in male critics' minds. Surely, Bradstreet tells her readers, her work will not "advance;" this is not the verse of a woman without ambition. It is the careful assessment of a gifted mind. Even her plea to rule out the traditionally male poetic subjects--war,

---

[28]Austin Warren, New England Saints (Ann Arbor: University of Michigan Press, 1956), 14.

royalty, conquest--in favor of direct feminine
experience went unheeded. For centuries, critics
focused only on her early apprentice period of
imitation, thereby rejecting her most personal and
intimate works. Her early exercises in Du Bartas and
Raleigh, common to male poets of her time, haunted
all critical judgements of her.

But Bradstreet speaks positively of the male artistic
contributions. Graciously, she allows them the
praise she knows full well they take. Men make and
enforce the rules of the literary, religious, and
secular societies. Bradstreet wants a fair place for
the woman artist in the literary world. She uses the
Greeks to build her case for women. After all, they
choose women to represent all "arts divine" and "made
poetry" Calliope's own child. Bradstreet knows that
an appeal to the authority of the Greeks will not
impress her Calvinistic audience, and quickly admits
the rapidity with which men will demolish her
argument. She lets "Greeks be Greeks, and women what
they are." But Bradstreet does not stop there. She
accords men their full recognition. "Men do best,
and women know it well/ Pre-eminence is all and each
is yours;/ Yet grant some small acknowledgement of
ours." These three prologue lines are crucial in
understanding Bradstreet's position. She did not
rebel against her society, because she accepted the
role of men in art and society, but she did want
recognition not only for herself but for other women
artists. The pronoun "ours" is the key; she
consistently uses it in both the first and second
editions. Only in the last stanza of the prologue
does she ask for a personal reward. "Give thyme or
parsley wreath, I ask no bays." Although she knows
she will never gain her society's acceptance as an
artist, she wants some recognition in the tradition
of poets: a simple, herb wreath. This plea for
recognition comes even in the prologue's final
couplet wherein Bradstreet acknowledges her poem's
imperfection but asks for its recognition
nonetheless. "This mean and unrefined ore of mine/
Will make your glist'ring gold but more to shine."

These are not the words of a humble, defenseless
woman as some critics suggest. The entire prologue
is meant to serve as introduction to a book of
verses; it is an appeal, both clear and traditional,

by the author for a proper audience for her poetry.
The poet's lines demonstrate a woman-artist generous
enough to praise men and wise enough to maintain a
sense of humor about her own simple, dramatic, and
sometimes didactic poetry. And her religion which
repressed her ambitions as a poet, also prompted her
to write. Denying herself an expressive outlet would
deny God's gift to her. Through Christian
affirmation, she developed her life and her poetry,
but she never forgot the attitude of her male-
dominated society towards women. While the world
gave her some popular recognition for her first
volume, she knew other women suffered as artists.
Even the English who welcomed her first work as a
curiosity were brutal to their own women poets.

In speaking of an English woman and contemporary of
Anne Bradstreet's, Lady Winchilsea, Virginia Woolf
tells us the story of how men chose to maintain women
"in a servile state."[29] Lady Winchilsea speaks of
her role as seventeenth century English lady. "They
[men] tell us we mistake our sex and way;/ Good
breeding, fashion, dancing, dressing, play/ Are
accomplishments we [women] should desire." Male
critics quickly labelled Lady Winchilsea a "blue
stocking with an itch for scribbling." Angry and
embittered, Winchilsea abandoned her active, public
role as poet and resumed a secluded "womanly" role,
but Bradstreet who never openly claimed society's
spotlight continued quietly writing. Winchilsea
faced brutal personal attack for her lack of
fertility as well. With no children to keep her
busy, her male critics carped, she naturally turned
to scribbling. No such argument threatened
Bradstreet who bore eight birds: "four cocks there
were and hens the rest."

In her careful verses, Bradstreet outlines the trials
and tribulations of bearing, nurturing, and sending
eight children to serve mankind. She expands these
themes in various ways; for example, children often
appear in her poetry as metaphors. In "The Author to

---

[29]Virginia Woolf, A Room of One's Own (New York:
Harcourt, Brace, Jovanovich, 1957), iv.

Her Book," Bradstreet expresses, in the terms least offensive to her male audience, her exasperation at suddenly finding that some man as put her "rambling brat (in print)" before she could dress him properly for a public visit. She suggests the consternation of mothers the world over whose unwashed child, still in dirty play clothes, is taken into a public place by a proud relative who is oblivious to the seemingly unimportant details of the child's disheveled appearance. She feels herself open to criticism for her apparent carelessness, and, at the same time, she is stunned by the man's failure to respect her feelings about the "trivia" she has been trained by her role to see as important.

> My rambling brat (in print) should mother call,
> I cast thee by as one unfit for light,
> Thy visage was so irksome in my sight;
> Yet being mine own, at length affection would
> Thy blemishes amend, if so I could.

Artist and mother both diligently try to cure their offspring's ills, so do they invariably succumb to their natural optimistic view that they can find positive solutions for all childish imperfections. But each knows in her heart even the best remedy sometimes fails.

> I washed thy face, but more defects I saw,
> And rubbing off a spot still made a flaw,
> I stretched thy joints to make thee even feet,
> Yet still thou run'st more hobbling than is meet.

Revise. Reform. Review. The best artistic or motherly effort eventually gives way to the reality of each child's and each poem's intrinsic strengths and weaknesses. As a woman Bradstreet accepts the imperfect nature of all created things, but she fully realizes this will in no way change the criticism she receives from men. As a woman she sees her life filled with unimportant, but unending details. Men will judge her by a tidy house, a scrubbed child, a hot meal. At the same time, they give little or no recognition to the importance of these endeavors as accomplishments worthy of recognition in comparison to the male accomplishments in the public world. They are different and not equal.

We see this clearly even in the words of a sympathetic twentieth century critic, Samuel Morison. Speaking from a man's point of view, Morison sees "The Author to Her Book" as "playful verse" that reflects Bradstreet's reaction to seeing her first edition "full of errata," but this interpretation does not consider the important lines that follow. Artistic criticism and human conflicts are both foes, and Bradstreet deals with them carefully. Wry humor is her secret and, if we are to judge from her male critics, overlooked weapon.[30]

As an artist-mother, Bradstreet knows the painful initiation each plain child or plain poem receives in the male-dominated society and the "carelessness" with which her poems were published gives her further evidence of her lack of power in the world of men and letters. She warns: "In this array 'mongst vulgars mayst thou roam/ In critics' hands, beware thou dost not come." Yet there is hardly a more delightful line affirming the singular, feminine creative role than her, "If for thy father asked, say, thou hadst none." Her brother-in-law's role as publisher was kind and compassionate, critics tell us. His role was also necessary, since no woman had the power to arrange such a thing. Through her work Anne Bradstreet declares the power of a woman's artistic creation, exclusive of the male influence.

While critics took pleasure in tracing her imitative verse (Ellis carefully compares Bradstreet's verses line by line with those of Sir Walter Raleigh and Guillarme Du Bartas's La Premiere Semaine, and Charles Eliot Norton reports that Bradstreet fails to enlighten the reader for "modes of existence or the social experience."[31]), few give Bradstreet credit for the poignant lyrical verse and sensitive prose that grew out of these modest beginnings, and which represent a personal, although fragmentary, account

---

[30]Morison, Intellectual Life, 119.

[31]The Poems of Anne Bradstreet, ed. Charles Eliot Norton (New York: Duedecimos, 1897), introduction.

of the inner world of a seventeenth century New England woman and artist. In another ironic twist, a major portion of the work that survived her home's burning on July 10, 1666 remained unknown outside her family for nearly two hundred years. This work, entitled the Andover Manuscript, appeared in John Harvard Ellis's 1867 edition of Anne Bradstreet poems, but typical male criticism and nineteenth century editing practices failed to address any of her feminist concerns properly or objectively. This essay and the selections included represent an attempt to correct the emphasis placed on the poet's earlier, more derivative poetry.

IV.

Anne Bradstreet through her subjects, the pain and sorrow that were part of the feminine role in life, presents us with a non-militant, even accepting picture of the distinct anguish felt by women who were reduced by their society to define themselves primarily according to their biological functions of nurturing and procreation. In their world such a devotion caused them to be intimate daily with illness and death and despair. The despondency and fear caused by pain of frequent childbirths and the sense of abandonment caused by extended absences of husbands in the active, "real" world created in a sensitive educated woman an almost intolerable burden of loneliness and isolation. The modern, lost, lonely woman looks pampered by comparison.

In her poem, "Before the Birth of One of My Children," the poet deals realistically and poignantly with the commonplace meeting with death that takes place each time she gives birth to a new child. "Adversity doth still our joys attend" notes the curious mixture of pain (death) and pleasure (a new life) that are inescapable. Even the choice of the line "The sentence past is most irrevocable" suggests a "penalty" each woman carries out as the ultimate price of her role as nurturing life-bearer. The immediacy and necessity of facing death are portrayed honestly as the poet asks her emerging child to let her many faults be "interred in my oblivious grave;" what then can the woman leave her child if she succumb to nature's sentence? Only the hope that in her verses the child may find the traces of his mother's love and artistic expression that are essential to the process of granting him life. "And if chance to thine eyes shall bring this verse/ With some sad sighs honour my absent hearse/ And kiss this paper for thy love's dear sake/ Who with salt tears this last farewell did take." In this work the poet clearly presents her sense of imminent death and the firm desire she will continue to live on in her verse.

This anguish, real and expressed, in a patriarchal society was not caused by a desire to be like men, but to find comfort in a religion which did not address itself to women's special faith-shaking experiences which were part of their daily lives. While the religion geared itself toward success, the women were cut off from that success in its worldly terms. Faced daily with illness and death, they tried to find evidence of God's special love and favor while facing each new day's tragedies. The work ethic which made prominent, successful worldly men surer of their salvation made women wonder whether they had God's concern or interest at all.

In the Tenth Muse such subjects are found in the final four poems. In "Flesh and the Spirit," Bradstreet chooses two sisters to speak for the classical conflict between soul and body developed by St. Paul. This poem, often hailed as a masterful interpretation, has another set of distinct possibilities. The world of the flesh, the world Bradstreet rejects, is the world filled with all the material tributes men offer each other.

> Dost honour like? acquire the same
> As some to their immortal fame.
> And trophies to thy name erect
> Which wearing time shall ne'er deject.

Like her "Flesh," Bradstreet rejects the masculine, materialistic world in favor of "Spirit" who turns from this world and seeks her rewards in heaven. Only when Bradstreet lets the spirit speak do we see a woman's perspective on her possible rewards revealed:

> The hidden manna I do eat
> The word of life it is my meat.
> My thoughts do yield me more content
> Than can thy hours in pleasure spent.

Each sister then leaves to the other the trophies of established male values: one, material and two, spiritual. Only in the spiritual world does the poet see any possible acknowledgement of her gifts. In her everyday life, denial was commonplace. In the eyes of others, she was a woman of comfortable means and high social position, but in her inner world, she sustained herself with dreams of paradise's golden streets and the possibility of release from sickness, separation, and infirmity.

In Several Poems, Rogers added thirteen short pieces found in the poet's private papers. All of these deal directly with Bradstreet's personal illnesses, her husband's continued absence, and the death of her grandchildren and daughter-in-law, Mercy. In these special poems commemorating the death of those close to her, Bradstreet shows a Christian feminist's passion for the preciousness of life, and the inevitability of each soul's returning to God. Still she mourns:

> Farewell dear babe, my heart's too much content,
> Farewell sweet babe, the pleasure of mine eye,
> Farewell fair flower that for a space was lent,
> Then ta'en away unto eternity.

In these poems commemorating the loss of a young child like Bradstreet's grand-daughter Elizabeth, we see the eternal Christian view, not merely a response to the frequency of infant mortality; we find an expression of the overwhelming sense of loss set against the need to accept God's providence.

At her daughter-in-law Mercy's death, she writes to her son Samuel, absent as his own father had so often been:

I lost a daughter dear, but thou a wife,
Who loved thee more (it seemed than her own life,
Thou being gone, she longer could not be,
Because her soul she'd sent along with thee.

The words bring Samuel solace, but for Ann Bradstreet
the painful loneliness of a woman's waiting for her
absent husband while suffering from childbirth pain
or some other "sore fit" or "fainting" was a
familiar reality of the woman's daily lot.

In the Andover Manuscript, her last personal and
private poems and messages, we see a Christian who
can lament and yet reconcile herself to personal
loss. Through her works she speaks clearly. In the
poem, "Upon the Burning of My House," Bradstreet
recalls the awful pain of awakening to the horrible
word, "Fire." Each painful moment becomes life-like
as the poet tells us of her sudden dash from her
beloved Andover home. In the darkness she stands
watching fire consume her treasures. She reports,
"And, when I could no longer look/ I blest his name
that gave and took." Initially, this experience
devastated Anne. We know from historical accounts
that she had already moved numerous times before
settling in Andover. Salem, Charlestown, Boston,
Cambridge, and Ipswich were all, at one time of
another, places where the Bradstreets lived. It was
here at Andover, however, that Anne made her special
home, the one that held her fondest memories. Her
losses were great. A careful inventory provided by
old records lists the family's worldly treasures: a
personal library of 800 volumes, the family
portraits, heirlooms, fine English furniture, and
regrettably, the poet's personal manuscripts. So
much evidence that might today shed light on her life
and work burned to ashes that single July night. In
time, Simon built Anne a finer, larger house, but,
for Anne, none could compare with the one that
burned.[32] In her poem, she details the extent of her
painful losses; she speaks of those precious moments
spent with family and friends that were synonymous

---

[32]Sarah Loring Bailey, Historical Sketches of
Andover (Boston: Houghton-Mifflin, 1880), 128-129.

with her destroyed home and of the special, personal mementos that are irreplacable. Only by the poem's end does she regain her witty and often practical touch. Then, she predicts her new home is, in fact, a heavenly one that is "purchased and paid for too/ By him who hath enough to do."

Bradstreet's preoccupation with birth, child raising, and home life continue even as her children grow. Her verses concern her children's safety on voyages, their sudden illnesses, and their religious salvation. She leaves them kind words and encourages them to seek God's kingdom in her "Religious Experiences," but she often admits her own "transgressions" and "vanities," lest they see her as dogmatic rather than a naturally imperfect mother. Of her long, persistent illnesses, she advises them to always remember each thing has some special purpose. Each illness, she reports, brings some good fortune through an answered prayer, so each seeming punishment brings some unique reward. In her discussion of sexual passion, she simply uses the word "heat," and when her children all leave her with an "empty nest," she prays they remember her kind words and deeds. In her letters to her husband Simon, we find her passionate and loving verses record her faithful devotion to him. Through all these works, we see a woman whose life took shape through obedience, passion, suffering, loneliness, joy, and, on occasion, natural beauty. We see her in a debilitating final illness as a woman who racked with pain still finds the presence to describe herself as "weary pilgrim, now at rest/ Hugs with delight his silent nest." Ready to give up her "corrupt carcass" so her new glorious body may arise; joyfully, she goes to Christ, her Saviour. It is the final poem, the final act of giving, the final act of love.

These works contain the real legacy that has too long been overlooked. Samuel Morison says it is "a curious fact that the historians of American literature, most of them New Englanders, rated Anne Bradstreet with an almost offensive condescension...."[33] The 1950's and 1960's saw little change as many American literature collections made brief or no mention of Bradstreet's poetry. In the 1970's, her work emerged occasionally alongside that of Edward Taylor, a "recognized" New England poet. Ann Bradstreet has, as yet, no impartial critical inquiry.

While Cotton Mather in his pompous seventeenth century euology of Bradstreet compares her to classical women, he never escapes the notion of her first being Governor Dudley's daughter and a "crown" to her father. Nowhere does he mention one specific work by the poet.[34] Even in Edward Phillips' notice, Anne Bradstreet is "a New England poetess," but not one of her non-historical poems receives mention.[35]

While earlier critics focused on Bradstreet's apprentice period of imitative works, later critics found her revelations of personal experiences unladylike. In a nineteenth century assessment of Bradstreet's work, the Duyckinck brothers criticize the poet for telling the whole truth "without any regard to the niceties or scruples of the imagination."[36] Their tone is negative, but inadvertently, they admitted, of course, Bradstreet was direct, honest, and original. In other words, Bradstreet cleverly adapted the much admired Puritan "plain style," but this fact was not recognized or appreciated because she was a woman. This type of

---

[33]Samuel Morison, _Master Builders of the Bay Colony_ (New York: Houghton-Mifflin, 1930), 331.

[34]Cotton Mather, _Magnalia Christi Americana_, Book ii, 17.

[35]Edward Phillips, _Theatrum Poetarum_ (London: Printed for Charles Smith, 1675), no page.

[36]Evert A. and George L. Duyckinck, _Cyclopaedia of American Literature_ (Philadelphia: Zell, 1875), I, 53.

criticism is all too common, and as a whole, it forms a three hundred year history of sexual criticism.

Terms such as imitative, limited, resigned, submissive, and cowardly too often find their way into Bradstreet criticisms.[37] Even her relationship to her Calvinistic beliefs received a different kind of criticism than that given to male Calvinistic poets. Her acceptance of disasters is labelled cowardly while her male counterparts received praise for the same attitudes. For example, Jonathan Edwards' ability to see the hand of God in events won him the description "saintly."[38] There must be an accurate accounting of the term "providence" and all it implied in Bradstreet's life and works: the positive, if not always understandable, act of God.

Male critics of the early 1980's suggest we must divorce Anne Bradstreet from all feminist concerns and view her critical comments as only jokes or light-hearted banter.[39] This presents us with a wonderfully ironic situation that shows stilted criticism still exists. When Bradstreet dealt with serious matters, her critics said she demonstrated a lack of taste. So through humor, a wry, self-deprecating art, she addressed the difficult feminist issues of her day without risking male wrath. Today, critics dismiss these remarks as non-essential to understanding her work; consequently, they disregard the fact Bradstreet used the only terms available to her as a woman. After three hundred years, they still do not understand the nature of her humor or what they perceive to be a joke.

---

[37]Randall Stewart, American Literature and Christian Doctrine (Baton Rouge: Louisiana State University Press, 1958), 13-14.

[38]Robert Spiller et. al., Literary History of the United States (New York: Macmillan, 1974), I.

[39]The Complete Poems of Anne Bradstreet, eds. Joseph McElrath, Jr. and Allan P. Robb (Boston: Twayne, 1981), xiii.

A careful reading of Bradstreet's work lets us share each aspect of the special legacy of a seventeenth century New England woman's inner world. The poet tells us much about her days, but still more, in regard to women, of ours.

This edition provides the student, the scholar, and interested reader with an accurate, modern version of those poems and prose selections which deal with Anne Bradstreet's inner feminist world. Thus, the focus is on the poet's perception of her life and role in seventeenth century America, a place wherein men designed both secular and religious life roles leading to successful worldly achievement and recognition, and women, regardless of their artistic talents, bore the rigors and tragedies of an often painful, lonely existence. Those works revealing the poet's inner world, a uniquely feminine sphere, deserve acceptance on their own merits; therefore, I selected materials that reflect those special concerns. Included are selections from the first and second editions of Anne Bradstreet's works, as well as the poet's work from the original Andover Manuscript, a body of work left by the poet to her children and treasured by her family privately for almost two centuries.

To establish as accurate an edition as possible, I removed seventeenth century spelling and printing accidentals; wherever possible, I left the poet's punctuation as it reflected her personal phrasing. I changed punctuation only to preserve the artist's own poetic sense or clarity. Hopefully, this method removed any seventeenth century barriers that prevent an interested reader from understanding and enjoying the works, and, at the same time, maintained the artist's unique quality of cohesive and rhythmic style.

The copy texts used for this edition are as follows:

Several Poems, the second edition, published in Boston in 1678, is the edition most closely associated with the poet; therefore, it is the primary copy text for applicable feminist works. This edition contains the poet's corrections of first edition works, a few minor line changes, and some additional poems found among her papers after her death. Although published posthumously, this edition represents the only one that we know the poet had any control over, limited though it was. Most critics believe that John Rogers, President of Harvard University, edited this version.

The two other principal editions are entitled The Tenth Muse Lately Sprung Up in America, the first edition of a literary work published that reflected the concerns of life in the new world, and a third edition published in Boston in 1758 without the poet or publisher's name. Since her brother-in-law, John Woodbridge, carried the original manuscript to England and arranged for its printing, Bradstreet had no control over first edition final editing, proofreading or printing. In the case of the third edition, the poet had no connection with the preparation or printing; this edition also omits many important characteristics of either of the two earlier editions.

These works are available at the Beinecke Library at Yale University and the Stevens Memorial Library at North Andover, Massachusetts. See listing of extant copies in the appendix.

All known Anne Bradstreet works from the Andover Manuscript appear in their entirety. This Manuscript, written partly in the poet's own hand, with the remaining sections copied by her son, Simon, from an original no longer believed in existence, is the other principal text. (A partial Latin transcription by the poet's grandson, Simon, also appears in the Manuscript.) To clarify unintelligible marks or words, the John Ellis edition of Anne Bradstreet's works served as source. This edition was the first to include the Andover Manuscript materials. The original Andover Manuscript is now at the Houghton Library, Harvard University, for conservation purposes.

There are several other nineteenth and twentieth century editions and collections of Anne Bradstreet's works and these appear in the Bibliography.

EDITING PRACTICES

In preparing this text, I modernized spelling, removed unnecessary capitals, wrote out all abbreviations, and regularized punctuation. For example, modern and, where appropriate, correct spellings appear: smote for smott, grief for greif, than for then. Old fashioned word forms appear in tact: whilst, lastest, and ye are frequent entries. Where a word meaning or spelling is unclear, a note provides information. In order to assist the reader in poetry selections, I used the following guidelines. Where the modern verb spelling does not add an inflection in current pronunciation, it appears in modern form: lived for liv'd, bowed for bow'd. Where the shorter form requires it, the original appears: show'st for showest, help'st for helpest. When Bradstreet wrote out the verb ending, her rhyme pattern consistently required the additional inflection. Since modern pronunciation sometimes precludes this, an accent(\) designates the additional inflection: thus, clothèd instead of clothed.

In capitalization, I preserved all those references to God such as Almighty, Eternal Being, Maker, and all references to important words such as Truth, Faith, Scriptures, Heaven, and Hell. Abbreviations such as &, wth, ye are written out as words. In both prose and poetry selections, Bradstreet's original punctuation appears. In other cases, I added marks where appropriate and sensible for a modern reading. In such matters, I paid close attention to the seventeenth century sentence sense and, particularly, to Bradstreet's rhythmic prose and poetry. For these reasons, all the poet's parentheses are in tact; the semi-colon clarifies involved phrasing rather than the full-stop intrusion of the period. Through this approach, I hopefully avoided the familiar editing trap of attempting to "improve" the artist's work and thereby destroy its own inherent qualities.

References to biblical passages, psalms, and special words are noted by an asterisk in the text. A brief explanation appears at the end of each work. Lengthy references to Bradstreet geneology and related matters may be found in the "Notes" section.

THE PROLOGUE

1

To sing of wars, of captains, and of kings,
Of cities founded, commonwealths begun,
For my mean pen are too superiour things:
Or how they all, or each, their dates have run
Let poets and historians set these forth,
My obscure lines shall not so dim their worth.

2

But when my wond'ring eyes and envious heart
Great Bartas sugared lines do but read o'er,
Fool I do grudge the Muses did not part
'Twixt him and me that overfluent store;
A Bartas can, do what a Bartas will
But simple I according to my skill.

3

From school boys' tongue no rhet'ric we expect,
Nor yet a sweet comfort from broken strings,
Nor perfect beauty, where's a main defect:
My foolish, broken blemished Muse so sings
And this to mend, alas, no art is able,
'Cause nature, made it so irreparable.

4

Nor can I, like that fluent sweet tongued Greek,
Who lisped at first, in future times speak plain,
By Art he gladly found what he did seek,
A full requital of his striving pain;
Art can do much, but this maxim's most sure:
A weak or wounded brain admits no cure.

5

I am obnoxious to each carping tongue
Who says my hand a needle better fits,
A poet's pen all scorn I should thus wrong,
For such despite thy cast on female wits:

If what I do prove well, it won't advance,
They'll say it's stol'n, or else it was by chance.

6

But sure the antique Greeks were far more mild
Else of our sex, why feigned they those nine
And poesy made, Calliope's own child;
So 'mongst the rest they placed the arts divine:
But this weak knot, they will full soon untie,
The Greeks did nought, but play the fools and lie.

7

Let Greeks be Greeks, and women what they are
Men have precedency and still excel,
It is but vain unjustly to wage war;
Men can do best, and women know it well
Pre-eminence is all and each is yours;
Yet grant some small acknowledgement of ours.

8

And oh ye high flown quills that soar the skies,
And ever with your prey still catch your praise,
If e'er you deign these lowly lines your eyes
Give thyme or parsley wreath, I ask no bays,
This mean and unrefined ure* of mine
Will make you[r] glist'ring gold, but more to shine.

A.B.

*ure: ore.

TO THE MEMORY OF MY DEAR AND EVER HONOURED
FATHER THOMAS DUDLEY, ESQUIRE, WHO DECEASED
JULY 31, 1653, AND OF HIS AGE, 77.

By duty bound, and not by custom led
To celebrate the praises of the dead,
My mournful mind, sore pressed, in trembling verse
Presents my lamentations at his hearse,
Who was my father, guide, instructor too,
To whom I ought whatever I could do;
Nor is't relation near by hand shall tie,
For who more cause to boast his worth than I?
Who heard or saw, observed or knew him better?
Or who alive than I, a greater debtor?
Let malice bite, and envy know its fill,
He was my father, and I'll praise him still;
Nor was his name, or life lead so obscure
That pity might some trumpeters procure,
Who after death might make him falsely seem
Such as in life, no man could justly deem;
Well known and loved, where e'er he lived, by most
Both in his native, and in foreign coast,
These to the world his merits could make known,
So needs to testimonial from his own;
But now or never I must pay my sum;
While others tell his worth, I'll not be dumb;
One of thy founders, him New England know,
Who stayed thy feeble sides when thou wast low,
Who spent his state, his strength, and years with
    care
That after-comers in them might have share;
True patriot of this little commonweal,
Who is't can tax thee ought, but for thy zeal?
Truth's friend thou wert, to errors still a foe,
Which caused apostates to malign so;
Thy love to true religion e'er shall shine,
My father's God, be God of me and mine;
Upon the earth he did not build his nest,
But as a pilgrim, what he had, possessed;
High thoughts he gave no harbor in his heart,
Nor honours puffed him up, when he had part:
Those titles loathed, which some too much do love,
For truly his ambition lay above;
His humble mind so loved humility,
He left it to his race for legacy:

3

And oft and oft, with speeches mild and wise,
Gave his in charge, that jewel rich to prize;
No ostentation seen in all his ways,
As in the mean ones, of our foolish days,
Which all they have, and more still set to view,
Their greatness may be judged by what they shew;
His thoughts were more sublime, his actions wise,
Such vanities he justly did despise;
Nor wonder 'twas, low things ne'er much did move
For he a mansion had, prepared above,
For which he sighed and prayed and longed full sore
He might be cloathed upon, for evermore;
Oft spake of death, and with a smiling cheer
He did exult his end was drawing near,
Now fully ripe, as shock of wheat that's grown,
Death as a sickle hath him timely mown,
And in celestial barn hath housed him high,
Where storms, nor show'rs, nor ought can damnify;
His generation served, his labours cease;
And to his fathers gathered is in peace;
Ah, happy soul, 'mongst saints and angels blest,
Who after all his toil, is now at rest;
His hoary head in righteousness was found,
As joy in Heaven on earth let praise resound;
Forgotten never be his memory,
His blessing rest on his posterity;
His pious footsteps followed by his race,
At last will bring us to that happy place
Where we with joy each other's face shall see,
And parted more by death shall never be.

4

HIS EPITAPH

Within this tomb a patriot lies
That was both pious, just and wise,
To truth a shield, to right a wall,
To sectaries a whip and maul,
A magazine of history,
A prizer of good company
In manners pleasant and severe
The good him loved, the bad did fear,
And when his time with years was spent
In some rejoiced, more did lament.

AN EPITAPH ON MY DEAR AND EVER HONOURED MOTHER,
MRS. DOROTHY DUDLEY, WHO DECEASED
DECEMBER 27, 1643, AND OF HER AGE, 61.

Here lies
A worthy matron of unspotted life,
    A loving mother and obedient wife,
A friendly neighbor, pitiful to poor,
Whom oft she fed, and clothèd with her store;
To servants wisely aweful, but yet kind,
And as they did, so they reward did find:
A true instructor of her family,
The which she ordered with dexterity,
The public meetings ever did frequent,
And in her closet constant hours she spent;
Religious in all her words and ways,
Preparing still for death, till end of days:
Of all her children, children lived to see,
Then dying, left a blessèd memory.

CONTEMPLATIONS

1

Some time now past in the autumnal tide,
When Phoebus wanted but one hour to bed,
The trees all richly clad, yet void of pride,
Where gilded o'er by his rich golden head.
Their leaves and fruits seemed painted, but was true
Of green, of red, or yellow, mixed hew,
Rapt were my senses at this delectable view.

2

I wist not what to wish, yet sure thought I,
If so much excellence abide below;
How excellent is he that dwells on high?
Whose power and beauty by his works we know.
Sure he is goodness, wisdom, glory, light,
That hath this under world so richly dight:
More Heaven than earth was here, no winter and no
    night.

3

Then on a stately oak I cast mine eye,
Whose ruffling top the clouds seemed to aspire;
How long since thou wast in thine infancy?
Thy strength, and stature, more thy years admire,
Hath hundred winters past since thou wast born?
Or thousand since thou brakest thy shell of horn,
If so, all these as nought, Eternity doth scorn.

4

Then higher on the glittering sun I gazed,
Whose beams was shaded by the leavie tree,
The more I looked, the more I grew amazed,
And softly said, what glory's like to thee?
Soul of this world, this universe's eye,
No wonder, some made thee a deity:
Had I not better known (alas) the same had I.

5

Thou as a bridegroom from thy chamber rushes,
And as a strong man, joys to run a race,

The morn doth usher thee, with smiles and blushes,
The earth reflects her glances in thy face.
Birds, insects, animals with vegative,
Thy heart from death and dullness doth revive:
And in the darksome womb of fruitful nature dive.

6

Thy swift annual, and diurnal course,
Thy daily straight, and yearly oblique path,
Thy pleasing fervor, and thy scorching force,
All mortals here the feeling knowledge hath.
Thy presence makes it day, thy absence night,
Quaternal seasons caused by thy might:
Hail creature, full of sweetness, beauty and delight.

7

Art thou so full of glory, that no eye
Hath strength, thy shining rays once to behold?
And is thy splendid throne erect so high?
As to approach it, can no earthly mould?
How full of glory then must thy Creator be?
Who gave this bright light luster unto thee:
Admired, adored, for ever, be that Majesty.

8

Silent alone, where none or saw, or heard,
In pathless paths I lead my wand'ring feet,
My humble eyes to lofty skies I reared
To sing some song, my mazed muse thought meet.
My great Creator I would magnify,
That nature had, thus decked liberally:
But Ah, and Ah, again, my imbecility!

9

I heard the merry grasshopper then sing,
The black-clad cricket, bear a second part,
They kept one tune, and played on the same string,
Seeming to glory in their little art.
Shall creatures abject, thus their voices raise?
And in their kind resound their Maker's praise:
Whilst I as mute, can warble forth no higher lays?

When present times look back to ages past,
And men in being fancy those are dead,
It makes things gone perpetually to last,
And calls back months and years that long since
    fled;
It makes a man more aged in conceit,
Than was Methuselah, or's grand-sire great:
While of their persons and their acts his mind doth
    treat.

11

Sometimes in Eden fair, he seems to be,
Sees glorious Adam there made lord of all,
Fancies the apple, dangle on the tree,
That turned his sovereign to a naked thrall.
Who like a miscreant's driven from the place,
To get his bread with pain, and sweat of face:
A penalty imposed on his backsliding race.

12

Here fits our grandame in retired place,
And in her lap, her bloody Cain new born,
The weeping imp oft looks her in the face,
Bewails his unknown hap, and fate forlorn;
His mother sighs to think of Paradise,
And how she lost her bliss, to be more wise,
Believing him that was, and is, father of lies.

13

Here Cain and Abel come to sacrifice,
Fruits of the earth, and fatlings each do bring,
On Abel's gift the fire descends from skies,
But no such sign on false Cain's offering:
With sullen hateful looks he goes his ways.
Hath thousand thoughts to end his brother's days,
Upon whose blood his future good he hopes to raise.

14

There Abel keeps his sheep, no ill he thinks,
His brother comes, then acts his fratricide,
The virgin earth, of blood her first draught drinks
But since that time she often hath been cloyed;

The wretch with ghastly face and dreadful mind,
Thinks each he sees will serve him in his kind,
Though none on earth but kindred near then could he
    find.

15

Who fancies not his looks now at the bar,
His face like death, his heart with horror fraught,
Nor malefactor ever felt like war,
When deep despair, with wish of life hath fought,
Branded with guilt, and crushed with treble woes,
A vagabond to Land of Nod he goes.
A city builds, that walls might him secure from foes.

16

Who thinks not oft upon the father's ages,
Their long descent, how nephews' sons they saw,
The starry observations of those sages,
And how their precepts to their sons were law,
How Adam sighed to see his progeny,
Cloathed all in his black sinful livery,
Who neither guilt, nor yet the punishment could fly.

17

Our life compare we with their length of days
Who to the tenth of theirs doth now arrive?
And though thus short, we shorten many ways,
Living so little while we are alive;
In eating, drinking, sleeping, vain delight
So unawares comes on perpetual night,
And puts all pleasures vain unto eternal flight.

18

When I behold the heavens as in their prime,
And then the earth (though old) still clad in green,
The stones and trees, insensible of time,
Nor age nor wrinkle on their front are seen;
If winter come and greenness then do fade,
A spring returns, and they more youthful made;
But man grows old, lies down, remains where once he's
    laid.

19

By birth more noble than those creatures all,
Yet seems by nature and by custom cursed,
No sooner born, but grief and care makes fall
That state obliterate he had at first:
Nor youth, nor strength, nor wisdom spring again,
Nor habitations long their names retain,
But in oblivion to the final day remain.

20

Shall I then praise the heavens, the trees, the
    earth
Because their beauty and their strength last longer
Shall I wish there, or never to had birth,
Because they're bigger, and their bodies stronger?
Nay, they shall darken, perish, fade and die,
And when unmade, so ever shall they lie,
But man was made for endless immortality.

21

Under the cooling shadow of a stately elm
Close sat I by a goodly river's side,
Where gliding streams the rocks did overwhelm,
A lonely place with pleasures dignified;
I once that loved the shady woods so well,
Now thought the rivers did the trees excel,
And if the sun would ever shine, there would I
    dwell.

22

While on the stealing stream I fixt mine eye,
Which to the longed for ocean held its course,
I marked, nor crooks, nor rubs that there did lie
Could hinder ought, but still augment its force:
O happy flood, quoth I, that holds thy race
Till thou arrive at thy beloved place,
Nor is it rocks or shoals that can obstruct thy
    pace.

23

Nor is't enough, that thou alone mayst slide,
But hundred brooks in thy clear waves do meet,
So hand in hand along with thee they glide

To Thetis' house, where all embrace and greet:
Thou emblem true, of what I count the best,
O could I lead my rivolets to rest,
So may we press to that vast mansion, ever blest.

24

Ye fish which in this liquid region 'bide,
That for each season, have your habitation,
Now salt, now fresh where you think best to glide
To unknown coasts to give a visitation,
In lakes and ponds, you leave your numerous fry,
So nature taught, and yet you know not why,
You wat'ry folk that know not your felicity.

25

Look how the wantons frisk to taste the air,
Then to the colder bottom straight they dive,
Eftsoon to Neptune's glassy hall repair
To see what trade they great ones there do drive,
Who forage o'er the spacious sea-green field,
And take the trembling prey before it yield,
Whose armour is their scales, their spreading fins
        their shield.

26

While musing thus with contemplation fed,
And thousand fancies buzzing in my brain,
The sweet-tongued Philomel perched o'er my head,
And chanted forth a most melodious strain
Which rapt me so with wonder and delight,
I judged my hearing better than my sight,
And wished me wings with her a while to take my
        flight.

27

O merry bird (said I) that fears no snares,
That neither toils nor hoards up in thy barn,
Feels no sad thoughts, nor cruciating cares
To gain more good, or shun what might thee harm
Thy clothes ne'er wear, thy meat is every where,
Thy bed a bough, thy drink the water clear,
Reminds not what is past, nor what's to come dost
        fear.

12

The dawning morn with songs thou dost prevent,
Sets hundred notes unto thy feathered crew,
So each one tunes his pretty instrument,
And warbling out the old, begin anew,
And thus they pass their youth in summer season,
Then follow thee into a better region,
Where winter's never felt by that sweet airy
    legion.

29

Man at the best a creature frail and vain,
In knowledge ignorant, in strength but weak,
Subject to sorrows, losses, sickness, pain,
Each storm his state, his mind, his body break,
From some of these he never finds cessation,
But day or night, within, without, vexation,
Troubles from foes, from friends, from dearest,
    near'st relation.

30

And yet this sinful creature, frail and vain,
This lump of wretchedness, of sin and sorrow,
This weather-beaten vessel wracked with pain,
Joys not in hope of an eternal morrow;
Nor all his losses, crosses and vexation,
In weight, in frequency and long duration
Can make him deeply groan for that divine
    translation.

31

The mariner that on smooth waves doth glide,
Sings merrily, and steers his bark with ease,
And if he had command of wind and tide,
And now become great master of the seas;
But suddenly a storm spoils all the sport,
And makes him long for a more quiet port,
Which 'gainst all adverse winds may serve for fort.

32

So he that saileth in this world of pleasure,
Feeding on sweets, that never bit of th' sour,
That's full of friends, of honour and of treasure,

Fond fool, he takes this earth ev'n for Heav'n's
    bower;
But sad affliction comes and makes him see
Here's neither honour, wealth, nor safety;
Only above is found all with security.

33

O Time the fatal wrack of mortal things,
That draws oblivion's curtains over kinds,
Their sumptuous monuments, men know them not,
Their names without a record are forgot,
Their parts, their ports, their pomp's all laid in
    th' dust,
Nor wit nor gold, nor buildings scape times rust;
But he whose name is graved in the white stone*
Shall last and shine when all of these are gone.

*Revelations 2:17.

14

THE FLESH AND THE SPIRIT

In secret place where once I stood
Close by the Banks of Lacrim flood
I heard two sisters reason on
Things that are past, and things to come;
One Flesh was called, who had her eye
On worldly wealth and vanity;
the other Spirit, who did rear
Her thoughts unto a higher sphere:
Sister quoth Flesh, what liv'st thou on,
Nothing but meditation?
Doth contemplation feed thee so
Regardlessly to let earth go?
Can speculation satisfy
Notion without reality?
Dost dream of things beyond the moon
And dost thou hope to dwell there soon?
Hast treasures there laid up in store
That all in th' world thou count'st but poor?
Art fancy sick or turned a sot
To catch at shadows which are not?
Come, come, I'll show unto thy sense,
Industry hath its recompense.
What canst desire, but you mayst see
True substance in variety?
Dost honour like? acquire the same,
As some of their immortal fame:
And trophies to thy name erect
Which wearing time shall ne'er deject.
For riches dost thou long full sore?
Behold enough of precious store.
Earth hath more silver, pearls and gold,
Than eyes can see, or hands can hold.
Affect's thou pleasure? take thy fill,
Earth hath enough of what you will.
Then let not go, what thou mayst find,
For things unknown, only in mind.
Spir.[it] Be still thou unregenerate part,
Disturb no more my settled heart,
For I have vowed (and so will do)
Thee as a foe, still to pursue.
And combat with thee will and must,
Until I see thee laid in th' dust.
Sisters we are, ye twins we be,
Yet deadly feud 'twixt thee and me;

For from one father are we not,
Thou by old Adam wast begot,
But my arise is from above,
Whence my dear Father I do love.
Thou speak'st me fair, but has more sore,
Thy flatt'ring shows I'll trust no more.
How oft thy slave, hast thou me made,
When I believed, what thou hast said,
And never had more cause of woe
Then when I did what thou bad'st do.
I'll stop mine ears at these thy charms,
And count them for my deadly harms.
Thy sinful pleasures I do hate,
Thy riches are to me no bait,
Thine honours do, nor will I love;
For my ambition lies above.
My greatest honour it shall be
When I am victor over thee,
And triumph shall, with laurel head,
When thou my captive shalt be led,
How I do live, thou need'st not scoff,
For I have meat thou know'st not of;
The hidden Manna I do eat,
The word of life it is my meat,
My thoughts do yield me more content
Than can thy hours in pleasure spent.
Nor are thy shadows which I catch,
Nor fancies vain at which I snatch,
But reach at things that are so high,
Beyond thy dull capacity;
Eternal substance I do see,
With which enriched I would be:
Mine eye doth pierce the heavens, and see
What is invisible to thee.
My garments are not silk nor gold,
Nor such like trash which earth doth hold,
But royal robes I shall have on,
More glorious than the glist'ring sun;
My crown not diamonds, pearls, and gold,
But such as angels' heads enfold.
The City where I hope to dwell,*
There's none on earth can parallel;
The stately walls both high and strong,
Are made of precious jasper stone;
The gates of pearl, both rich and clear,
And angels are for porters there;
The streets thereof transparent gold,
Such as no eye did e'er behold,

A crystal river there doth run,
Which doth proceed from the Lamb's throne:
Of life, there are the waters sure,
Which shall remain for ever pure,
Nor sun, nor moon, they have no need,
For glory doth from God proceed:
No candle there, nor yet torch light,
For there shall be no darksome night.
From sickness and infirmity,
Forevermore they shall be free,
Nor withering age shall e'er come there,
But beauty shall be bright and clear;
This City pure is not for thee,
For things unclean there shall not be:
If I of Heaven may have my fill,
Take thou the world, and all that will.

*Revelations 21: 10-27 and 22: 1-5.

THE VANITY OF ALL WORLDLY THINGS

As he said vanity, so vain say I,
Oh! vanity, O vain all under sky;
Where is the man can say, lo I have found*
On brittle earth a consolation sound?
What is't in honour to be set on high?
No, they like beasts and sons of men shall die:
And whilst they live, how oft doth turn their fate,
He's now a captive, that was king of late.
What is't in wealth, great treasures to obtain?
No, that's but labour, anxious care and pain,
He heaps up riches, and he heaps up sorrow,
It's his to-day, but who's his heir to-morrow?
What then? Content in pleasures canst thou find,
More vain than all, that's but to grasp the wind.
The sensual senses for a time they please,
Meanwhile the conscious rage, who shall appease?
What is't in beauty? No that's but a snare,
They're foul enough to-day, that once were fair.
What is't in flow'ring youth, or manly age?
The first is prone to vice, the last to rage.
Where is it then, in wisdom, learning arts?
Sure if on earth, it must be in those parts:
Yet these the wisest man of men did find
But vanity, vexation of mind.
And he that knows the most, doth still bemoan
He knows not all that here is to be known.
What is it then, to do as Stoics tell,
Nor laugh, nor weep, let things go ill or well.
Such Stoics are but stocks, such teaching vain,
While man is man, he shall have ease or pain.
If not in honour, beauty, age nor treasure,
Nor yet in learning, wisdom, youth nor pleasure,
Where shall I climb, sound, seek, search or find
That summum bonum which may stay my mind?
There is a path, no vulture's eye hath seen,
Where lion fierce, nor lion's whelps have been,
Which leads unto that living crystal fount,
Who drinks thereof, the world doth nought account
The depth and sea have said tis not in me,
With pearl and gold, it shall not valued be.
For sapphire, onyx, topaz who would change:
It's hid from eyes of men, they count it strange.
Death and destruction the same hath heard,

18

But where and what it is, from heaven's declared,
It brings to honour, which shall ne'er decay,
It stores with wealth which time can't wear away.
It yieldeth pleasures far beyond conceit,
And truly beautifies without deceit,
Nor strength, nor wisdom nor fresh youth shall fade
Nor death shall see, but are immortal made.
This pearl of price, this tree of life, this spring
Who is possessed of, shall reign a king.
Nor change of state, nor cares shall ever see,
But wear his crown unto eternity:
This satiates the Soul, this stays the mind,
And all the rest, but vanity we find.

*Ecclesiastes 25.

19

THE AUTHOR TO HER BOOK

Thou ill-formed offspring of my feeble brain,
Who after birth didst by my side remain,
Till snatched from thence by friends, less wise than
    true,
Who thee abroad, exposed to public view,
Made thee in rags, halting to th' press to trudge,
Where errors were not lessened (all may judge)
At thy return my blushing was not small,
My rambling brat (in print) should mother call,
I cast thee by as one unfit for light.
Thy visage was so irksome in my sight;
Yet being mine own, at length affection would
Thy blemishes amend, if so I could:
I washed thy face, but more defects I saw,
And rubbing off a spot, still made a flaw.
I stretched thy joints to make thee even feet,
Yet still thou run'st more hobbling than is meet;
In better dress to trim thee was my mind,
But nought save home-spun cloth, i'th' house I find
In this array, 'mongst vulgars mayst thou roam
In critics' hands, beware thou dost not come;
And take thy way where yet thou art not known,
If for thy father asked, say, thou hadst none:
And for thy mother, she alas is poor,
Which caused her thus to send thee out of door.

UPON A FIT OF SICKNESS, ANNO. 1632

Twice ten years old, not fully told
    since nature gave me breath,
My race is run, my thread is spun,
    lo, here is fatal Death;
All men must die, and so must I,
    this cannot be revoked;
For Adam's sake, this word God spake
    when he so high provoked;
Yet live I shall, this life's but small,
    in place of highest bliss,
Where I shall have all I can crave,
    no life is like to this;
For what's this life, but care and strife?
    since first we came from womb,
Our strength doth waste, our time doth haste,
    and then we go to the tomb;
O bubble blast, how long can'st last?
    that always art a breaking,
No sooner blown, but dead and gone,
    ev'n as a word that's speaking:
O whilst I live, this grace me give,
    I doing good may be,
Then death's arrest, I shall count best,
    because it's thy decree;
Bestow much cost, there's nothing lost,
    to make Salvation sure,
O great's the gain, though got with pain,
    comes by profession pure;
The race is run, the field is won,
    the victory's mine I see,
Forever know, thou envious foe,
    the foil belongs to thee.

UPON SOME DISTEMPER OF BODY

In anguish of my heart replete with woes,
And wasting pains, which best my body knows,
In tossing slumbers on my wakeful bed,
Bedrenched with tears that flowed from mournful head
Till nature had exhausted all her store,
Then eyes lay dry, disabled to weep more;
And looking up unto his throne on high,
Who sendeth help to those in misery;
He chased away those clouds, and let me see
My anchor cast i' the vale with safety;
He eased my soul of woe, my flesh of pain,
And brought me to the shore from troubled main.

BEFORE THE BIRTH OF ONE OF MY CHILDREN

All things within this fading world hath end,
Adversity doth still our joys attend;
No ties so strong, no friends so dear and sweet,
But with death's parting blow is sure to meet.
The sentence past is most irrevocable,
A common thing, yet oh inevitable;
How soon, my dear, death may my steps attend,
How soon it may be thy lot to lose thy friend,
We both are ignorant, yet love bids me
These farewell lines to recommend to thee,
That when the knot's untied that made us one,
I may seem thine, who in effect am none;
And if I see not half my days that's due,
What nature would, God grant to yours and you;
The many faults that well you know I have,
Let be interred in my oblivious grave;
If any worth or virtue were in me,
Let that live freshly in thy memory
And when thou feel'st no grief, as I no harms,
Yet love thy dead, who long lay in thine arms:
And when thy loss shall be repaid with gains,
Look to my little babes my dear remains;
And if thou love thy self, or loved'st me
These O protect from step dame's injury;
And if chance to thine eyes shall bring this verse,
With some sad sighs honour my absent hearse;
And kiss this paper for thy love's dear sake,
Who with salt tears this last farewell did take.

A.B.

TO MY DEAR AND LOVING HUSBAND

If ever two were one, then surely we;
If ever man were loved by wife, then thee;
If ever wife was happy in a man,
Compare with me ye women if you can;
I prize thy love more than whole mines of gold,
Or all the riches that the East doth hold;
My love is such that rivers cannot quench,
Nor ought but love from thee, give recompense;
Thy love is such I can no way repay,
The heavens reward thee manifold I pray;
Then while we live, in love let's so persevere,
That when we live no more, we may live ever.

A LETTER TO MY HUSBAND, ABSENT UPON
PUBLIC EMPLOYMENT

My head, my heart, mine eyes, my life, nay more,
My joy, my magazine of earthly store,
If two be one, as surely thou and I,
How stayest thou there, whilst I at Ipswich lie?
So many steps, head from the heart to fever
If but a neck, soon should we be together:
I like the earth this season, mourn in black,
My sun is gone so far in's zodiac,
Whom whilst I 'joyed, nor storms, nor frosts I felt,
His warmth such frigid colds did cause to melt;
My chilled limbs now numbed lie forlorn;
Return, return, sweet sol from capricorn;
In this dead time, alas, what can I more
Than view those fruits which through thy heat I bore?
Which sweet contentment yield me for a space,
True living pictures of their father's face;
O strange effect! Now thou art Southward gone,
I weary grow, the tedious day so long;
But when thou Northward to me shalt return,
I with my sun may never set, but burn
Within the cancer of my glowing breast,
The welcome house of him my dearest guest;
Where ever, ever stay, and go not thence,
Till nature's sad decree shall call thee hence;
Flesh of thy flesh, bone of thy bone,
I here, thou there, yet both but one.

A.B.

PHOEBUS MAKE HASTE. . . . .

ANOTHER

Phoebus make haste, the day's too long, be gone,
The silent night's the fittest time for moan;
But stay this once, unto my suit give ear,
And tell my griefs in either hemisphere:
(And if the whirling of thy wheels don't drowned)
The woeful accents of my doleful sound,
If in thy swift carrier thou canst make stay,
I crave this boon, this errand by the way,
Commend me to the man more loved than life,
Show him the sorrows of his widowed wife;
My dumpish thoughts, my groans, my brakish tears,
My sobs, my longing hopes, my doubting fears,
And if he love, how can he there abide?
My interest's more than all the world beside;
He that can tell the stars of ocean sand,
Or all the grass that in the meads do stand,
The leaves in th' woods, the hail or drops or rain,
Or in a corn-field number every grain,
Or every mote that in the sun-shine hops,
May count my sighs, and number all my drops:
Tell him, the countless steps that thou dost trace,
That once a day, thy spouse thou mayst embrace;
And when thou canst not treat by loving mouth,
Thy rays afar, salute her from the South.
But for one month I see no day (poor soul)
Like those far situate under the pole,
Which day by day long wait for thy arise,
O how they joy when thou dost light the skies;
O Phoebus, had'st thou but thus long from thine
Restrained the beams of thy beloved shine,
At thy return, if so thou could'st or durst
Behold a chaos blacker than a confused matter,
His little world's a fathom under water,
Nought but the fervor of his ardent beams
Hath power to dry the torrent of these streams;
Tell him I would say more, but cannot well,
Oppressed minds abruptest tales do tell;
Now post with double speed, mark what I say,
By all our loves conjure him not to stay.

26

AS LOVING HIND. . . .

ANOTHER

As loving hind that (hartless) wants her deer,
Scuds through the woods and fern with hark'ning ear,
Perplexed, in every bush and nook doth pry,
Her dearest deer, might answer ear or eye;
So doth my anxious soul, which now doth miss,
A dearer dear (far dearer heart) than this;
Still wait with doubts, and hopes, and failing eye,
His voice to hear, or person to discry;
Or as the pensive dove doth all alone
(On withered bough) most uncouthly bemoan
The absence of her love, and loving mate,
Whose loss hath made her so unfortunate:
Ev'n thus do I, with many a deep sad groan
Bewail my turtle true, who now is gone,
His presence and his safe return, still wooes,
With thousand doleful sighs and mournful coos;
Or as the loving mullet, that true fish,
Her fellow lost, nor joy nor life do with,
But launches on that shore, there for to die,
Where she her captive husband doth espy;
Mine being gone, I lead a joyless life,
I have a loving sphere, yet seem no wife:
But worst of all, to him can't steer my course,
I here, he there, alas, both kept by force:
Return my dear, my joy, my only love,
Unto thy hind, thy mullet, and thy dove,
Who neither joys in pasture, house nor streams,
The substance gone, O me, these are but dreams;
Together at one tree, oh let us browse,
And like two turtles roost within one house,
And like the mullets in one river glide,
Let's still remain but one, till death divide.

                    Thy loving love and dearest dear,
                    At home, abroad, and everywhere.

                                        A.B.

MOST TRULY HONOURED AND AS TRULY DEAR

Most truly honoured, and as truly dear,
If worth in me, or ought I do appear,
Who can of right better demand the fame?
Than may your worthy self from whom it came.
The principle might yield a greater sum,
Yet handled ill, amounts but to this crumb;
My stock's so small, I know not how to pay,
My bond remains in force unto this day;
Yet for part payment take this simple mite,
Where nothing's to be had kings lose their right;
Such is my debt, I may not say forgive,
But as I can, I'll pay it while I live:
Such is my bond, none can discharge but I,
Yet paying is not paid until I die.

                                        A.B.

28

IN REFERENCE TO MY CHILDREN, 23 JUNE, 1659*

I had eight birds hatched in one nest,
Four cocks there were, and hens the rest,
I nursed them up with pain and care,
Nor cost, nor labour did I spare,
Till at the last they felt their wing;
Mounted the trees and learned to sing;
Chief of the brood then took his flight,
To regions far, and left me quite:
My mournful chirps I after send,
Till he return, or I do end,
Leave not thy nest, thy dam and sire,
Fly back and sing amidst this choir;
My second bird did take her flight,
And with her mate flew out of sight;
Southward they both their course did bend,
And seasons twain they there did spend:
Till after blown by southern gales,
They northward steered with fillèd sails;
A prettier bird was no where seen,
Along the beach among the treen;
I have a third of color white,
On whom I placed no small delight;
Coupled with mate loving and true,
Hath also bid her dam adieu:
And where Aurora first appears,
She now hath perched, to spend her years;
One to the Academy flew
To chat among the learned crew:
Ambition moves still in his breast
That he might chant above the rest,
Striving for more than to do well,
That nightingales he might excel;
My fifth, whose down is yet scarce gone
Is 'mongst the shrubs and bushes flown,
And as his wings increase in strength,
On higher boughs he'll perch at length;
My other three, still with me nest,
Until they're grown, then as the rest,
Or here or there, they'll take their flight,
As is ordained, so shall they light;
If birds could weep, then would my tears
Let others know what are my fears
Lest this my brood some harm should catch,
And be surprised for want of watch,

Whilst pecking corn, and void of care
They fall un'wares in fowler's snare:
Or whilst on trees they sit and sing,
Some untoward boy at them do fling:
Or whilst allured with bell and glass,
The net be spread, and caught, alas;
Or least by lime twigs they be foiled,
Or by some greedy hawks be spoiled;
O would my young, ye saw my breast,
And knew what thoughts there sadly rest,
Great was my pain when I you bred,
Great was my care, when I you fed,
Long did I keep you soft and warm,
And with my wings kept off all harm,
My cares are more, and fears than ever,
My throbs such now, as 'fore were never:
Alas my birds, you wisdom want,
Of perils you are ignorant,
Oft times in grass, on trees, in flight,
Sore accidents on you may light;
O to your safety have an eye
So happy may you live and die:
Meanwhile my days in tunes I'll spend,
Till my weak lays with me shall end;
In shady woods I'll sit and sing,
And things that past, to mind I'll bring;
Once young and pleasant, as you are,
But former toys (no joys) adieu;
My age I will not once lament,
But sing, my time so near is spent;
And from the top bough take my flight,
Into a country beyond sight,
Where old ones, instantly grow young,
And there with seraphims set song:
No seasons cold, nor storms they see;
But spring lasts to eternity,
When each of you shall in your nest
Among your young ones take your rest,
In chirping language, oft them tell,
You had a dam that loved you well,
That did what could be done for young,
And nursed you up till you were strong,
And 'fore she once would let you fly,
She showed you joy and misery;
Taught what was good, and what was ill,
What would save life, and what would kill?
Thus gone, amongst you I may live,
And dead, yet speak, and counsel give:

Farewell my birds, farewell adieu,
I happy am, if well with you.

*Please see "Notes."

IN MEMORY OF MY DEAR GRAND-CHILD
ELIZABETH BRADSTREET, WHO DECEASED
AUGUST, 1665, BEING A YEAR AND HALF OLD*

1

Farewell dear babe, my heart's too much content,
Farewell sweet babe, the pleasure of mine eye,
Farewell fair flower that for a space was lent,
Then ta'en away unto eternity.
Blest babe why should I once bewail thy fate,
Or sigh the days so soon were terminate;
Since thou art settlèd in an everlasting state.

2

By nature trees do rot when they are grown.
And plumbs and apples thoroughly ripe do fall,
And corn and grass are in their season mown,
And time brings down what is both strong and tall.
But plants new set to be eradicate,
And buds new blown, to have so short a date,
Is by his hand alone that guides nature and fate.

*Elizabeth was the eldest child of Samuel and Mercy
Bradstreet.

32

IN MEMORY OF MY DEAR GRAND-CHILD ANNE BRADSTREET,
WHO DECEASED JUNE 20, 1669, BEING THREE YEARS
AND SEVEN MONTHS OLD*

With troubled heart and trembling hand I write,
The Heavens have changed to sorrow my delight;
How oft with disappointment have I met,
When I on fading things my hopes have set?
Experience might 'fore this have made me wise,
To value things according to their price:
Was ever stable joy yet found below?
Or perfect bliss without mixture of woe;
I knew she was but as a withering flower,
That's here to-day, perhaps gone in an hour;
Like as a bubble, or the brittle glass,
Or like a shadow turning as it was;
More fool that I to look on that was lent,
As if mine own, when thus impermanent;
Farewell dear child, thou ne'er shall come to me,
But yet a while, and I shall go to thee;
Mean time, my throbbing heart's cheered up with this:
Thou with thy Saviour art in endless bliss.

*Anne was the eldest living child of Simon and Mercy
Bradstreet.

ON MY DEAR GRAND-CHILD SIMON BRADSTREET, WHO DIED
ON 16 NOVEMBER 1669, BEING BUT ONE MONTH,
AND ONE DAY OLD*

No sooner came, but gone, and fallen asleep,
Acquaintance short, yet parting caused us weep,
Three flowers, two scarcely blown, the last i' th'
bud,
Cropped by the Almighty's hand; yet is he good,
With dreadful awe before him let's be mute,
Such was his will, but why, let's not dispute,
With humble hearts and mouths put in the dust;
Let's say he's merciful, as well as just.
He will return, and make up all our losses,
And smile again, after our bitter crosses;
Go pretty babe, go rest with sisters twain
Among the blest in endless joys remain.

                                          A.B.

*Simon was the fourth child of Samuel and Mercy
Bradstreet.

34

TO THE MEMORY OF MY DEAR DAUGHTER-IN-LAW, MRS.
MERCY BRADSTREET, WHO DECEASED SEPTEMBER 6, 1669,
IN THE TWENTY EIGHTH YEAR OF HER AGE*

And live I still to see relations gone,
And yet survive to sound this wailing tone;
Ah, woe is me, to write thy funeral song,
Who might in reason yet have lived long,
I saw the branches lopped, the three now fall,
I stood so nigh, it crushed me down withal;
My bruised heart lies sobbing at the root,
That thou dear son hath lost both tree and fruit:
Thou then on seas sailing to foreign coast;
Was ignorant what riches thou hadst lost;
But ah too soon those heavy tidings fly,
To strike thee with amazing misery;
Oh how I sympathize with thy sad heart,
And in thy griefs still bear a second part:
I lost a daughter dear, but thou a wife,
Who loved thee more (it seemed) than her own life;
Thou being gone, she longer could not be,
Because her soul she'd sent along with thee;
One week she only past in pain and woe,
And then her sorrows all at once did go;
A babe she left before, she soared above,
The fifth and last pledge of her dying love,
E're nature would, it hither did arrive,
No wonder it no longer did survive;
So with her children four, she's now at rest,
All freed from grief (I trust) among the blest;
She one hath left, a joy to thee and me,
The heavens vouchsafe she may so ever be,
Cheer up (dear son) thy fainting bleeding heart,
In him alone, that caused all this smart;
What though thy strokes full sad and grievous be,
He knows it is the best for thee and me.

                                        A.B.

*Please refer to "Notes."

TO MY DEAR CHILDREN

This book by any yet unread,
I leave for you when I am dead,
That being gone, here you may find
What was your living mother's mind.
Make use of what I leave in love
And God shall bless you from above.

A.B.

My dear children,--

I, knowing by experience that the exhortations of
parents take most effect when the speakers leave to
speak, and being ignorant whether on my death bed I
shall have opportunity to speak to any of you much
less to all, thought it the best whilst I was able to
compose some short matters (for what else to call
them I know not) and bequeath to you, that when I am
no more with you, yet I may be daily in your
rememberance (although that is the least in my aim in
what I now do) but that you may gain some spiritual
advantage by my experience. I have not studied in
this you read to show my skill, but to declare the
Truth, not to set forth my self, but the Glory of
God. If I had minded the former it had been perhaps
better pleasing to you, but seeing the last is the
best, let it be best pleasing to you.

The method I will observe shall be this--I will begin
with God's dealing with me from my childhood to this
day.

In my young years, about 6 or 7 as I take it, I began
to make conscience of my ways, and what I knew was
sinful as lying, disobedience to parents, etcetera, I
avoided it. If at any time I was overtaken with the
like evils, it was a great trouble. I could not be
at rest 'till by prayer I had confessed it unto God.

36

I was also troubled at the neglect of private duties, though too often tardy that way. I also found much comfort in reading the Scriptures, especially those places I thought most concerned my condition, and as I grew to have more understanding, so the more solace I took in them.

In a long fit of sickness which I had on my bed, I often communed with my heart, and made my supplication to the most high who set me free from that affliction.

But as I grew up to be about 14 or 15 I found my heart more carnal, and fitting loose from God, vanity and the follies of youth take hold of me.

About 16, the Lord laid his hand sore upon me and smote me with the small pox. When I was in my affliction, I besought the Lord, and confessed my pride and vanity and he was entreated of me, and again restored me. But I rendered not to him according to the benefit received.

After a short time I changed my condition and was married and came into this country, where I found a new world and new manners, at which my heart rose. But after I was convinced it was the way of God, I submitted to it and joined to the church at Boston.

After some time I fell into a lingering sickness like a consumption, together with a lameness, which correction I saw the Lord sent to humble and try me and do me good: and it was not altogether ineffectual.

It pleased God to keep me a long time without a child which was a great grief to me, and cost me many prayers and tears before I obtained one, and after him gave me many more, of whom I now take the care, that as I have brought you into the world, and with great pains, weakness, cares, and fears brought you to this, I now travail in birth again of you till Christ be formed in you.

Among all my experiences of God's gracious dealings with me I have constantly observed this, that he hath never suffered me long to sit loose from him, but by one affliction or other hath made me look home, and search what was amiss--so usually thus it hath been with me that I have no sooner felt my heart out of order, but I have expected correction for it, which most commonly hath been upon my own person, in sickness, weakness, pains, sometimes on my soul, in doubts and fears of God's displeasure, and my sincerity towards him. Sometimes he hath smote a child with sickness, sometimes chastened by losses in estate, and these times (through his great mercy) have been the times of my greatest getting and advantage, yea I have found them the times when the Lord hath manifested the most love to me. Then have I gone to searching, and have said with David, Lord search me and try me, see what ways of wickedness are in me, and lead me in the way everlasting: and seldom or never but I have found either some sin I lay under which God would have reformed, or some duty neglected which he would have performed. And by his help I have laid vows and bonds upon my soul to perform his righteous commands.

If at any time you are chastened of God, take it as thankfully and joyfully as in greatest mercies. For if ye be his, ye shall reap the greatest benefit by it. It hath been no small support to me in times of darkness, when the Almighty hath hid his face from me, that yet I have had abundance of sweetness and refreshment after affliction and more circumspection in my walking after I have been afflicted. I have been with God like an untoward child, that no longer than the rod has been on my back (or at least in sight) but I have been apt to forget him and my self too. Before I was afflicted I went astray, but now I keep thy statutes.

I have had great experience of God's hearing my prayers, and returning comfortable answers to me, either in granting the thing I prayed for, or else in satisfying my mind without it; and I have been confident it hath been from him, because I have found my heart through his goodness enlarged in thankfulness to him.

I have often been perplexed that I have not found that constant joy in my pilgrimage and refreshing which I supposed most of the servants of God have, although he hath not left me altogether without the witness of his Holy Spirit, who hath oft given me his

word and set to his seal that it shall be well with
me. I have sometimes tasted of that hidden manna
that the world knows not, and have set up my
Ebenezer, and have resolved with my self that against
such a promise, such tastes of sweetness, the gates
of Hell shall never prevail. Yet have I many
sinkings and droopings, and not enjoyed that felicity
that sometimes I have done. But when I have been in
darkness and seen no light, yet have I desired to
stay my self upon the Lord. And, when I have been in
sickness and pain, I have thought if the Lord would
but lift up the light of his countenance upon me,
although he ground me to powder, it would be but
light to me. Yea, often have I thought were it Hell
itself and could there find the love of God toward
me, it would be a Heaven. And, could I have been in
Heaven without the love of God, it would have been a
Hell to me. For, in Truth, it is the absence and
presence of God that makes Heaven or Hell.

Many times hath Satan troubled me concerning the
verity of the Scriptures, many times by atheism. How
could I know whether there was a God if I never saw
any miracles to confirm me, and those which I read
of, how did I know, but they were feigned. That
there is a God my reason would soon tell me by the
wondrous works that I see, the vast frame of the
Heaven and the earth, the order of all things, night
and day, summer and winter, spring and autumn, the
daily providing for this great household upon the
earth, the preserving and directing of all to its
proper end. The consideration of these things would
with amazement certainly resolve me that there is an
Eternal Being.

But how should I know he is such a God as I worship
in Trinity, and such a Saviour as I rely upon?
Though this hath thousands of times been suggested to
me, yet God hath helped me over. I have argued thus
with my self. That there is a God I see. If ever
this God hath revealed himself, it must be in his
word, and this must be it or none. Have I not found
that operation by it that no humane invention can
work upon the soul? Hath not judgements befallen
diverse who have scorned and contend it? Hath it not
been preserved through all ages maugre all the
heathen tyrants and all of the enemies who have
opposed it? Is there any story but that which shows

the beginnings of times, and how the world came to be as we see? Do we not know the prophecies in it fulfilled which could not have been so long foretold by any but God himself?

When I have got over this block, then have I another put in my way. That admit this be the true God whom we worship, and that be his word, yet why may not the popish religion be the right? They have the same God, the same Christ, the same word. They only interpret it one way, we another.

This hath sometimes stuck with me, and more it would, but the vain fooleries that are in their religion, together with their lying miracles, and cruel persecutions of the saints, which admit were they as they term them, yet not so to be dealt withall.

The consideration of these things and many the like would soon turn me to my own religion again.

But some new troubles I have had since the world has been filled with blasphemy, and sectaries, and some who have been accounted sincere Christians have been carried away with them, that sometimes I have said, "Is there faith upon the earth?" And I have not known what to think; but then I have remembered the words of Christ that so it must be, and that, if it were possible, the very elect should be deceived. "Behold," saith our Saviour, "I have told you before," that hath stayed my heart, and I can now say, "Return, O my soul, to thy rest, upon this rock Christ Jesus will I build my faith, and if I perish, I perish." But I know all the powers of Hell shall never prevail against it. I know whom I have trusted, and whom I have believed, and that he is able to keep that I have committed to his charge.

Now to the King, immortal, eternal, and invisible, the only wise God, be honor and glory for ever and ever. Amen.

This was written in much sickness and weakness, and is very weakly and imperfectly done; but if you can pick any benefit out of it, it is the mark which I aimed at.

OCCASIONAL MEDITATIONS

Here follow several occasional meditations.

1

By night when others soundly slept
And had at once both east and rest,
My waking eyes were open kept,
And so to lie I found it best.

2

I sought him whom my soul did love,
With tears I sought him earnestly,
He bowed his ear down from above,
In vain I did not seek or cry.

3

My hungry soul he filled with good,
He in his bottle put my tears,
My smarting wounds washed in his blood,
And banished thence my doubts and fears.*

4

What to my Saviour shall I give,
Who freely hath done this for me?
I'll serve him here whilst I shall live,
And love him to eternity.

*Psalm 56:8.

FOR DELIVERANCE FROM A FEVER

When sorrows had begirt me round, *Bind around*
    And pains within and out,
When in my flesh no part was found, *nothing spared*
    Then didst thou rid me out. *cleanse*

My burning flesh in sweat did boil,
    My aching head did break,
From side to side for ease I toil,
    So faint I could not speak.

Beclouded was my soul with fear
    Of thy displeasure sore,
Nor could I read my evidence
    Which oft I read before.

Hide not thy face from me, I cried,
    From burnings keep my soul,
Thou knowst my heart, and hast me tried;
    I on thy mercies roll.

O, heal my soul, thou knowst I said,
    Though flesh consume to nought,
What though in dust it shall be laid,
    To glory 't shall be brought.

Thou heardst, thy rod thou didst remove,
    And spared my body frail,
Thou showst to me thy tender love,
    My heart no more might quail.

O praises to my mighty God,
    Praise to my Lord, I say,
Who hath redeemed my soul from pit, *Hell*
    Praises to him for aye!* *Ever*

*Psalm 22:8 or 37:5.

42

FROM ANOTHER SORE FIT

In my distress I sought the Lord
When nought on Earth could comfort give,
And when my soul these things abhored,
Then Lord, thou said'st unto me, "Live."

Thou knowest the sorrows that I felt,
My complaints and groans were heard of thee,
And how in sweat I seemed to melt,
Thou help'st and thou regardest me.

My wasted flesh thou didst restore,
My feeble loins didst gird with strength,*
Yea when I was most low and poor,
I said I shall praise thee at length.

What shall I render to my God
For all his bounty showed to me,
Even for his mercies in his rod,
Where pity most of all I see.

My heart I wholly give to thee,
O make it fruitful, faithful Lord,
My life shall dedicated be
To praise in thought, in deed, in word.

Thou knowst no life I did require
Longer then shall thy name to praise,
Nor ought on earth worthy desire,
In drawing out these wretched days.

Thy name and praise to celebrate,
O Lord, for aye is my request
O, grant I do it in this state,
And then with thee which is the best.

*Proverbs 31:17.

DELIVERANCE FROM A FIT OF FAINTING

Worthy art thou, O Lord of praise,
  But ah! it's not in me;
My sinking heart I pray thee raise,
  So shall I give it thee.

My life as spider's web's cut off,
  Thus fainting have I said,
And living man no more shall see,
  But be in silence laid.

My feeble spirit thou didst revive,
  My doubting thou did chide,
And though as dead mad'st me alive,
  I hear a while might 'bide.

Why should I live but to thy praise,
  My life is hid with thee;
O Lord, no longer be my days,
  Then I may fruitful be.

MEDITATIONS

WHEN MY SOUL HATH BEEN REFRESHED WITH THE CONSOLATIONS WHICH THE WORLD KNOWS NOT

Lord, why should I doubt any more when thou hast given me such assured pledges of thy love. First thou art my Creator, I thy creature; thou my master, I thy servant. But hence arises not my comfort: Thou art my father, I thy child. "Ye shall my sons and daughters," saith the Lord Almighty. Christ is my brother; I ascend unto my father and your father, unto my God and your God. But lest this should not be enough, thy maker is thy husband. Nay more, I am a member of his Body, he my head. Such privileges had not the word of Truth made them known, who or where is the man that durst in his heart have presumed to have thought it? So wonderful are these thoughts that my spirit fails in me at the consideration thereof, and I am confounded to think that God who hath done so much for me should have so little from me. But this is my comfort. When I come into Heaven, I shall understand perfectly what he hath done for me, and then shall I be able to praise him as I ought. Lord, having this hope, let me purify my self as thou are pure, and let me be no more afraid of death, but even desire to be dissolved and be with thee which is best of all.

WHAT GOD IS LIKE TO HIM, I SERVE,
JULY 8, 1656

I had a sore fit of fainting which lasted 2 or 3 days, but not in that extremity which at first it took me, and so much the sorer it was to me because my dear husband was from home (who is my chiefest comforter on earth) but my God who never failed me, was not absent but helped me, and graciously manifested his love to me, which I dare not pass by without remembrance, that it may be a support to me when I shall have occasion to read this hereafter, and to others that shall read it when I shall possess that I now hope for, that so they may be encouraged to trust him who is the only portion of his servants.

O Lord, let me never forget thy goodness, nor question thy faithfulness to me, for thou art my God thou hast said, and shall not I believe it?

Thou hast given me a pledge of that inheritance thou hast promised to bestow upon me. O never let Satan prevail against me, but strengthen my faith in thee, 'till I shall attain the end of my hopes, even the salvation of my soul.

Come Lord Jesus, come quickly.

What God is like to him I serve,
    What Saviour like to mine?
O never let me from thee swerve,
    For truly I am thine.

My thankful mouth shall speak thy praise,
    My tongue shall talk of thee,
On high my heart O do thou raise,
    For what thou'st done for me.

Go, worldlings, to your vanities,
    And heathen to your gods;
Let them help in adversities,
    And sanctify their rods.

My God, he is not like to yours,
    Your selves shall judges be;
I find his love, I know his pow'r,
    A succourer of me.

He is not man that he should lie,
    Nor son of man to unsay,
His word he plighted hath on high,
    And I shall live for aye.

And for his sake that faithful is,
    That died but now doth live,
The first and last that lives for aye,
    Me lasting life shall give.

MY SOUL, REJOICE THOU IN THY GOD

My soul, rejoice thou in thy God,
  Boast of him all the day,
Walk in his law and kiss his rod.
  Cleave close to him alway.

What though thy outward man decay,
  Thy inward shall wax strong,
Thy body vile it shall be changed,
  And glorious made ere long.

With angels' wings thy soul shall mount
  To bliss unseen by eye,
And drink at unexhausted fount
  Of joy unto eternity.

Thy tears shall all be dried up,
  Thy sorrows all shall fly;
Thy sins shall never be summoned up,
  Nor come in memory.

Then shall I know what thou hast done
  For me, unworthy me,
And praise thee shall even as I ought,
  For wonders that I see.

Base world, I trample on thy face,
  Thy glory I despise,
No gain I find in ought below,
  For God hath made me wise.

Come Jesus quickly, Blessed Lord,
  Thy face when shall I see?
O let me count each hour a day
  'Till I dissolvèd be.

AFTER MUCH WEAKNESS

August 28, 1656

After much weakness and sickness when my spirits were worn out, and many times my faith weak likewise, the Lord was pleased to uphold my drooping heart, and to manifest his love to me, and this is that which stays my soul that this condition that I am in is the best for me, for God doth not afflict willingly, nor take delight in grieving the children of men; he hath no benefit in my adversity, nor is he the better for my prosperity, but he doth it for my advantage, and that I may be a gainer by it. And if he knows that weakness and a frail body is the best to make me a vessel fit for his use, why should I not bare it, not only willingly but joyfully? The Lord knows I dare not desire that health that sometimes I have had, lest my heart should be drawn from him and set upon the world.

Now I can wait, looking every day when my Saviour shall call for me. Lord grant that while I live I may do that service I am able in this frail body, and be in continual expectation of my change, and let me never forget thy great love to my soul so lately expressed, when I could lie down and bequeath my soul to thee, and death seemed no terrible thing. O let me ever see thee that art invisible, and I shall not be unwilling to come though by so rough a messenger.

A SORE SICKNESS AND WEAKNESS

May 11, 1657

I had a sore sickness and weakness took hold of me
which hath by fits lasted all this spring till this
11 May; yet hath my God given me many a respite, and
some ability to perform the duties I owe to him, and
the work of my family.

Many a refreshment have I found in this my weary
pilgrimage, and in this valley of Baca many pools of
water. That which now I chiefly labour for is a
contented, thankful heart under my affliction and
weakness, seeing it is the will of God it should be
thus. Who am I that I should repine at his pleasure,
especially seeing it is for my spiritual advantage.
For I hope my soul shall flourish while my body
decays, and the weakness of this outward man shall be
a means to strengthen my inner man.*

Yet a little while and he that shall come will come
and will not tarry.

*Psalm 84:5,6.

AS SPRING AND SUMMER DOTH SUCCEED

May 13, 1657

As spring the winter doth succeed,
And leaves the naked trees do dress,
The earth all black is clothed in green,
At sunshine each their joy express.

My sun's returned with healing wings,
My soul and body doth rejoice,
My heart exults and praises sings
To him that heard my wailing voice.

My winter's past, my storms are gone,
And former clouds seem now all fled;
But, if they must eclipse again,
I'll run where I was succoured.

I have a shelter from the storm,
A shadow from the fainting heat;
I have access unto his throne,
Who is a God so wondrous great.

O hast thou made my pilgrimage
Thus pleasant, fair, and good;
Blessed me in youth and elder age,
Baca made a springing flood.*

I studious am, what I shall do
To show my duty with delight?
All I can give is but thine own,
And at the most a simple mite.

*Psalm 84:6.

IT PLEASED GOD TO VISIT ME

September 30, 1657

It pleased God to visit me with my old distemper of weakness and fainting, but not in that sore manner sometimes he hath. I desire not only willingly but thankfully to submit to him, for I trust it is out of his abundant love to my straying soul which in prosperity is too much in love with the world. I have found by experience I can no more live without correction than without food. Lord, with thy correction give instruction and amendment, and then thy strokes shall be welcome. I have not been, but have rather been preserved with sugar than brine; yet will he preserve me to his heavenly kingdom.

Thus (dear children) have yet seen the many sicknesses and weaknesses that I have passed through to the end that, if you meet with the like, you may have recourse to the same God who hath heard and delivered me and will do the like for you if you trust in him; and no, when he shall deliver you out of distress, forget not to give him thanks, but to walk more closely with him than before. This is the desire of your loving mother.

A.B.

UPON MY SON SAMUEL HIS GOING FOR ENGLAND, NOVEMBER 6, 1657*

Thou mighty God of sea and land
I here resign into thy hand
The son of prayers, of vows, of tears,
The child I stayed for many years.
Thou heard'st me then, and gav'st him me,
Hear me again, I give him thee.
He's mine, but more O Lord, thine own,
For sure thy grace on him is shown.
No friend I have like thee to trust,
For mortal helps are brittle dust.
Preserve, O Lord, from storms and wrack,
Protect him there and bring him back,
And if thou shalt spare me a space
That I again may see his face,
Then shall I celebrate thy praise,
And bless the sor't even all my days.
If otherwise I go to rest,
Thy will be done, for that is best.
Persuade my heart, I shall him see
Forever happifièd with thee.

*See Notes under "In Reference to My Children."

53

IT HATH PLEASED THE LORD

May 11, 1661

It hath pleased God to give me a long time of respite
for these four years that I have had no great fit of
sickness but this year, from the middle of January
'till May, I have been by fit very ill and weak. The
first of this month I have a fever seated upon me
which, indeed, was the longest and sorest that ever I
had, lasting four days, and the weather being very
hot made it the more tedious; but it pleased the Lord
to support my heart in his goodness, and to hear my
prayers, and to deliver me out of adversity. But,
alas! I cannot render unto the Lord according to all
his loving kindness, nor take the cup of salvation
with thanksgiving as I ought to do. Lord, thou that
knowest all things knowest that I desire to testify
my thankfulness not only in word, but in deed, that
my conversation may speak that thy vows are upon me.

MY THANKFUL HEART

IN CELEBRATION OF MY HUSBAND'S RECOVERY
FROM ILLNESS

May 11, 1661

My thankful heart with glorying tongue
    Shall celebrate thy name,
Who hath restored, redeemed, recured
    From sickness, death and pain.

I cried thou seem'st to make some stay,
    I sought more earnestly;
And in due time thou succour'st me,
    And send'st me help from high.

Lord, whilst my fleeting time shall last
    Thy goodness let me tell.
And new experience I have gained,
    My future doubts repel.

An humble, faithful life, O Lord,
    Forever let me walk,
Let my obedience testify,
    My praise lies not in talk.

Accept, O Lord, my simple might
    For more I cannot give,
What thou bestow'st I shall restore,
    For of thine alms I live.

FOR THE RESTORATION OF MY DEAR HUSBAND
FROM A BURNING AGUE,* JUNE, 1661

When fears and sorrows me beset
    Then didst thou rid me out,
When heart did faint and spirits quail
    Thou comforts me about.*

Thou raised him up I feared to loose,
    Regav'st me him again;
Distempers thou didst chase away,
    With strength did him sustain.

My thankful heart, with pen record
    The goodness of thy God,
Let thy obedience testify,
    He taught thee by his rod.

And with his staff did thee support,
    That thou by both mayst learn,
And 'twixt the good and evil way,
    At last, thou might'st discern.

Praises to him who hath not left
    My soul as destitute,
Nor turned his ear away from me,
    But granted hath my suit.

*ague: fever
*Psalm 71:21.

UPON MY DAUGHTER HANNAH WIGGIN HER RECOVERY FROM A DANGEROUS FEVER

Blest be thy name, who didst restore
    To health my daughter dear,
When death did seem even to approach
    And life was ended near.

Grant she remember what thou'st done
    And celebrate thy praise,
And let her conversation say
    She loves thee all thy days.

ON MY SON'S RETURN OUT OF ENGLAND, JULY 17, 1661*

All praise to him who hath now turned
My fears to joys, my sighs to song,
My tears to smiles, my sad to glad.
He's come for whom I waited long.

Thou didst preserve him as he went,
In raging storms didst safely keep,
Didst that ship bring to quiet port,
The other sank low in the deep.*

From dangers great thou didst him free
Of pirates who were near at hand,
And order'st so the adverse wind
That he before them got to land.

In country strange thou didst provide,
And friends raised him in every place
And countries of sundry sorts,
From such as 'fore ne'er saw his face.

In sickness when he lay full sore
His help and his physician wert;
When royal ones that time did die,*
Thou healed'st his flesh and cheered his heart.

From troubles and encumbers thou
Without (all fraud) didst set him free,
That without scandal he might come
To th' land of his nativity.

On eagle's wings him hither brought*
Through want and dangers manifold,
And thus hath granted my request
That I thy mercies might behold.

O help me pay my vows O Lord,
That ever I may thankful be,
And may put him in mind of what
Thou'st done for him, and so for me.

In both our hearts erect a frame
Of duty and of thankfulness,
That all thy favors great received
Our upright walking may express.

O Lord, grant that I may never forget thy loving
kindness in this particular, and how graciously thou
has answered my desires.

*Please refer to "Notes."

UPON MY DEAR AND LOVING HUSBAND HIS
GOING INTO ENGLAND, JANUARY 16, 1661*

O thou most high who rulest all
    And hear'st the prayers of thine;
O hearken Lord unto my suit
    And my petition sign.

Into thy everlasting arms
    Of mercy I commend
Thy servant Lord. Keep and preserve
    My husband, my dear friend.

At thy command O Lord he went,
    Nor nought could keep him back;
Then let thy promise joy his heart,
    O help and not be slack.

Uphold my heart in thee O God,
    Thou art my strength and stay;
Thou seest how weak and frail I am,
    Hide not thy face away.

I in obedience to thy will
    Thou knowest did submit;
I was my duty so to do
    O Lord accept of it.

Unthankfulness for mercies past
    Impute thou not to me;
O Lord thou know'st my weak desire
    Was to sing praise to thee.

Lord be thou pilot of the ship
    And send them prosperous gales;
In storms and sickness Lord preserve,
    Thy goodness never fails.

Unto thy work he hath in hand
    Lord grant thou good success,
And favour in their eyes to whom
    He shall make his address.

Remember Lord thy folk whom thou
    To wilderness have brought;
Let not thine own inheritance
    Be sold away for nought.

But tokens of thy favour give,
    With joy send back my dear,
That I and all thy servants may
    Rejoice with heavenly cheer.

Lord let my eyes see once again
    Him whom thou gavest me,
That we together may sing praise
    Forever unto thee.

And the remainder of our days
    Shall consecrated be,
With an engaged heart to sing
    All praises unto thee.

*The actual sailing date was February 11, 1662.

IN MY SOLITARY HOURS IN MY
DEAR HUSBAND'S ABSENCE

O Lord, thou hear'st my daily moan,
    And seest my dropping tears.
My troubles all are thee before,
    My longings and my fears.

Thou hitherto hast been my God,
    Thy help my soul hath found.
Though loss and sickness me assailed
    Though I've kept my ground.

And thy abode thou'st made with me,
    With thee my soul can talk;
In secret places, thee I find
    When I do kneel or walk.

Though husband dear be from me gone
    Whom I do love so well,
I have a more beloved one
    Whose comforts far excel.

O stay my heart, on thee my God,
    Uphold my fainting soul;
And when I know not what to do
    I'll on thy mercies roll.*

My weakness thou dost know full well,
    Of body and of mind.
I in this world no comfort have,
    But what from thee I find.

*Psalm 22:8; 37:5.

IN THANKFUL ACKNOWLEDGEMENT FOR THE
LETTERS I RECEIVED FROM MY HUSBAND
OUT OF ENGLAND

O thou that hear'st the prayers of thine
And 'mongst them hast regarded mine,
Hast heard my cries and seen my tears,
Hast known my doubts and all my fears.
Thou hast relieved my fainting heart
Nor paid me after my desert;
Thou hast to shore him safely brought
For whom I thee so oft besought;
Thou wast the pilot to the ship
And raised him up when he was sick;
And hope thou'st given of good success,
In this his business and address,
And that thou wilt return him back
Whose presence I so much do lack;
For all these mercies I thee praise
And so desire ev'n all my days.

IN THANKFUL REMEMBERANCE FOR MY
DEAR HUSBAND'S SAFE ARRIVAL,
SEPTEMBER 3, 1662

What shall I render to thy name
    Or how thy praises speak?
My thanks how shall I testify?
    O Lord thou know'st I'm weak,
I owe so much, so little can
    Return unto thy Name,
Confusion seizes on my soul
    And I am filled with shame;
O thou that hearest prayers Lord,
    To thee shall come all flesh;
Thou hast me heard and answered,
    My 'plaints have had access;
What did I ask for but thou gav'st?
    What could I more desire?
But thankfulness even all my days
    I humbly this require.
Thy mercies Lord have been so great
    In number numberless,
Impossible for to recount
    Or any way express.
O help thy saints that sought thy face
    T' return unto thee praise,
And walk before thee as they ought,
    In strict and upright ways.

FOR MY DEAR SON SIMON BRADSTREET*

Parents perpetuate their lives in their posterity, and their manners, in their imitation. Children do naturally rather follow the failings than the virtues of their predecessors, but I am persuaded better things of you. You once desired me to leave something for you in writing that you might look upon, when you should see me no more; I could think of nothing more fit for you nor of more ease to my self than these short meditations following. Such as they are I bequeath them to you; small legacies are accepted by true friends, much more by dutiful children. I have avoided encroaching upon others' conceptions because I would leave you nothing but mine own, though in value they fall short of all in this kind, yet I presume they will be better prized by you for the author's sake. The Lord bless you with grace here and crown you with glory hereafter, that I may meet you with rejoicing at that great day of appearing, which is the continual prayer, of

your affectionate mother,

A.B.

March 20, 1664

*The following selections are from the Andover Manuscript in the poet's own hand writing.

MEDITATIONS DIVINE AND MORAL

1

There is no object that we see, no action that we do,
no good that we enjoy, no evil that we feel, or fear,
but we may make some spiritu[a]l advantage of all and
he that makes such improvement is wise as well as
pious.

2

Many can speak well, but few can do well. We are
better scholars in the theory than the practic part,
but he is a true Christian that is a proficient in
both.

3

Youth is the time of getting, middle age of
improving, and old age of spending; a negligent youth
is usually attended by an ignorant middle age, and
both by an empty old age; he that hath nothing to
feed on but vanity and lies must needs lie down in
the bed of sorrow.

4

A ship that bears much sail, and little or no
ballast, is easily overset; and that man whose head
hath great abilities and his heart little or no grace
is in danger of foundering.

5

It is reported the peacock that priding him self in
his gay feathers, he ruffles them up; but spying his
black feet, he soon lets fall his plumes, so he that
glories in his gifts and adornings should look upon
his corruptions, and that will damp his high
thoughts.

The finest bread hath the least bran, the purest honey, the least wax, and the sincerest Christian the least self love.

The hireling that labours all the day, comforts him self that when night comes he shall both take his rest and receive his reward; the painful Christian that hath wrought hard in God's vineyard and hath born the heat and drought of the day, when he perceives his sun apace to decline and the shadows of his evening to be stretched out, lifts up his head with joy, knowing his refreshing is at hand.

Downy beds make drowsy persons, but hard lodging keeps the eyes open. A prosperous state makes a secure Christian, but adversity makes him consider.

Sweet words are like honey: a little may refresh, but too much gluts the stomach.

Diverse children have their different natures: some are like flesh which nothing but salt will keep from putrefaction, some again like tender fruits that are best preferred with sugar; those parents are wise that can fit their nurture according to their nature.

That town which thousands of enemies without hath not been able to take hath been delivered up by one traitor within, and that man which all the temptations of Satan without could not hurt hath been foiled by one lust within.

Authority without wisdom is like a heavy axe without edge, fitter to bruise than polish.

The reason why Christians are so loath to exchange this world for a better is because they have more sense than faith; they see what they enjoy; they do but hope for that which is to come.

14

If we had not winter the spring would not be so pleasant; if we did not sometimes taste of adversity, prosperity would not be so welcome.

15

A low man can go upright under that door where a taller is glad to stoop; so a man of weak faith and mean abilities may undergo a cross more patiently than he that excells him, both in gifts and graces.

16

That house which is not often swept makes the cleanly inhabitant soon loath it, and that heart which is not continually purifying it self is no fit temple for the spirit of God to dwell in.

17

Few men are so humble as not to be proud of their abilities, and nothing will abase them more than this: --What hast thou, but what thou hast received? Come give an account of thy stewardship.

18

He that will undertake to climb up a steep mountain with a great burden on his back will find it a wearisome if not an impossible task; so he that thinks to mount to heaven clogged with the cares and riches of this life, 'tis no wonder if he faint by the way.

19

Corn, till it have passed through the mill and been ground to powder, is not fit for bread. God so deals with his servants; he grinds them with grief and pain till they turn to dust, and then they are fit manchet for his Mansion.

20

God hath suitable comforts and supports for his children according to their several conditions if he will make his face to shine upon them; he then makes them lie down in green pastures and leads them besides the still waters; if they stick in deep mire and clay, and all his waves and billows go over their heads, he then leads them to the rock which is higher than they.

21

He that walks among briars and thorns will be very careful where he sets his foot. And he that passes through the wilderness of this world had need ponder all his steps.

22

Want of prudence as well as piety hath brought men into great inconveniencies, but he that is well stored with both seldom is so insnared.

23

The skillful fisher hath his several baits for several fish, but there is a hook under all; Satan that great Angler hath his sundry baits for sundry tempers of men, which they all catch greedily at, but few perceives the hook till it be too late.

24

There is no new thing under the sun; there is nothing that can be said or done, but either that or something like it hath been both done and said before.

25

An aching head requires a soft pillow, and a drooping heart a strong support.

A sore finger may disquiet the whole body, but an
ulcer within destroys it. So an enemy without may
disturb a commonwealth, but dissentions within over
throw it.

27

It is a pleasant thing to behold the light, but sore
eyes are not able to look upon it; the pure heart
shall see God, but the defiled in conscience shall
rather choose to be buried under rocks and mountains
than to behold the presence of the Lamb.

28

Wisdom with inheritance is good, but wisdom without
inheritance is better than an inheritance without
wisdom.

29

Lightning doth usually precede thunder, and storms
rain; and strokes do not often fall till after
threatening.

30

Yellow leaves argue want of sap and gray hairs want
of moisture. So dry and sapless performances are
symptoms of little spiritual vigor.

31

Iron till it be thoroughly heat is uncapable to be
wrought, so God sees good to cast some men into the
furnace of affliction and then beats them on his
anvil into that frame he pleases.

32

Ambitious men are like hops that never rest climbing
so long as they have any thing to stay upon, but take
away their props and they are of all, the most
dejected.

Much labour wearies the body, and many thoughts
oppress the mind; man aims at profit by the one and
content in the other, but often misses both and
finds nothing but vanity and vexation of spirit.

Dim eyes are the concomitants of old age, and short
sightedness in those that are eyes of a republic
foretells a declining state.

We read in Scripture of three sorts of arrows: the
arrow of an enemy, the arrow of pestilence, and the
arrow of a slanderous tongue; the two first kill the
body, the last the good name; the two former leave a
man when he is once dead, but the last mangles him in
his grave.

Some labourers have hard hands, and old sinners have
brawny consciences.

Wickedness comes to its height by degrees. He that
dares say of a less sin, is it not a little one will
ere long say of a greater, Tush, God regards it not.

Some children are hardly weaned although the teat be
rubbed with wormwood or mustard, they will wipe it
off, or else suck down sweet and bitter together; so
is it with some Christians; let God embitter all the
sweets of this life, that so they might feed upon
more substantial food, yet they are so childishly
sottish that they are still hugging and sucking these
empty breasts, that God is forced to hedge up their
way with thorns or lay affliction on their loines
that so they might shake hands with the world, before
it bid them farewell.

A prudent mother will not clothe her little child
with a long and cumbersome garment; she easily
foresees what events it is like to produce, at the
best, but falls and bruises, or perhaps somewhat
worse; much more will the all wise God proportion his
dispensations according to the stature and strength
of the person he bestows them on. Large endowments
of honour, wealth, or a healthful body would quite
over throw some weak Christian, therefore God cuts
their garments short, to keep them in such a trim
that they might run the ways of his commandment.

40

The spring is a lively emblem of the resurrection:
after a long winter we see the leaveless tree and dry
stock (at the approach of the sun) to resume their
former vigor and beauty in a more ample manner than
what they lost in the autumn; so shall it be at that
great day after a long vacation, when the Sun of
righteousness shall appear; those dry bones shall
arise in far more glory than that which they lost at
their creation, and in this transcends the spring,
that their leaf shall never fail nor their sap
decline.

41

A wise father will not lay a burden on a child of
seven years old which he knows is enough for one of
twice his strength; much less will our heavenly
Father (who knows our mold) lay such afflictions upon
his weak children as would crush them to dust, but
according to the strength he will proportion the
load; as God hath his little children so he hath his
strong men, such as are come to a full stature in
Christ, and many times he imposes weighty burdens on
their shoulders, and yet they go upright under them;
but it matters not whether the load be more or less
if God afford his help.

42

I have seen an end of all perfection (said the royal
prophet);* but he never said, I have seen an end of
all sinning; what he did say may be easily said by

many, but what he did not say, cannot truly be
uttered by any.

43

Fire hath its force abated by water, not by wind, and
anger must be allayed by cold words and not by
blustering threats.

44

A sharp appetite and a thorough concoction is a sign
of an healthful body, so a quick reception and a
deliberate cogitation argues a sound mind.

45

We often see stones hang with drops not from any
innate moisture but from a thick air about them; so
may we sometime see marble hearted sinners seem full
of contrition; but it is not from any dew of grace
within, but from some black clouds that impends them
which produces these sweating effects.

46

The words of the wise, sath* Soloman, are as nails
and as goads, both used for contrary ends: the one
holds fast, the other puts forward; such should be
the precepts of the wise masters of assemblies to
their hearers, not only to bid them hold fast the
form of sound doctrine, but also, so to run that they
might obtain.*

47

A shadow in the parching sun and a shelter in a
blustering storm are of all seasons the most welcome.
So a faithful friend in time of adversity is, of all
other, most comfortable.

48

There is nothing admits of more admiration than God's
various dispensation of his gifts among the sons of
men, betwixt whom he hath put so vast a disproportion
that they scarcely seem made of the same lump or
sprung out of the loins of Adam; some set in the

highest dignity, that mortality is capable of, and some gain so base, that they are viler than the earth, some so wise and learned, that they seem like angels among men, and some again, so ignorant and sottish that they are more like beasts than men, some pious saints, some incarnate devils, some exceeding beautiful and some extremely deformed. Some so strong and healthful that their bones are full of marrow and their breasts of milk, and some again so weak and feeble, that while they live, they are accounted among the dead, and no other reasons can be given of all this but so it pleased him, whose will is the perfect rule of righteousness.

49

The treasures of this world may well be compared to husks for they have no kernel in them, and they that feed upon them may soon stuff their throats but cannot fill their bellies; they may be choaked by them but cannot be satisfied with them.

50

Sometimes the sun is only shadowed by a cloud, that we cannot see his luster, although we may walk by his light; but when he is set, we are in darkness till he arise again. So God doth sometime veil his face but for a moment that we cannot behold the light of his countenance, as at some other time; yet he affords so much light as may direct our way, that we may go forwards to the city of habitation, but when he seems to set and be quite gone out of sight, then must we needs walk in darkness and see no light; yet then must we trust in the Lord and stay upon our God, and when the morning (which is the appointed time) is come the Sun of righteousness will arise with healing in his wings.

51

The eyes and the ears are the inlets or doors of the soul through which innumerable objects enter, yet is not that spacious room filled, neither doth it ever say it is enough; but like the daughters of the horseleech, cries, give, give,* and which is most strange, the more it receives, the more empty it finds it self, and sees an impossibility ever to be filled, but by him, in whom all fullness dwells.

52

Had not the wisest of men taught us this lesson, that all is vanity and vexation of spirit, yet our own experience would soon have spelled it out; for what do we obtain of all these things, but it is with labour and vexation? When we enjoy them it is with vanity and vexation, and if we lose them then they are less than vanity and more than vexation, so that we have good cause often to repeat that sentence, vanity of vanities, vanity of vanities, all is vanity.

53

He that is to sail into a far country, although the ship, cabin, and provision be all convenient and comfortable for him, yet he hath no desire to make that his place of residence but longs to put in at that port where his business lies; a Christian is sailing through this world unto his heavenly country, and here he hath many conveniences and comforts, but he must beware of desiring to make this the place of his abode, lest he meet with such tossings that may cause him to long for shore before he sees land. We must therefore be here as strangers and pilgrims, that we may plainly declare that we seek a city above and wait all the days of our appointed time till our change shall come.

54

He that never felt what it was to be sick or wounded doth not much care for the company of the physician or surgeon, but if he preceive a malady that threatens him with death, he will gladly entertain him whom he slighted before; so he that never felt the sickness of sin, nor the wounds of a guilty conscience, cares not how far he keeps from him that hath skill to cure it; but when he finds his diseases to disrest him, and that he must needs perish if he have no remedy will unfeignedly bid him welcome that brings a plaster for his fore or a cordial for his fainting.

75

55

We read of ten lepers that were cleansed, but of one
that returned thanks;* we are more ready to receive
mercies than we are to acknowledge them; men can use
great importunity when they are in distresses and
show great ingratitude after their successes, but he
that ordereth his conversation aright will glorify
him that heard him in the day of his trouble.

The remembrance of former deliverance is a great
support in present distresses; he that delivered me,
sath* David, from the paw of the lion and the paw of
the bear will deliver me from this uncircumcised
Philistine; and he that hath delivered me, saith
Paul, will deliver me. God is the same yesterday,
today, and for ever; we are the same that stand in
need of him, today as well as yesterday, and so shall
for ever.

Great receipts call for great returns: the more that
any man is intrusted with all, the larger his
accounts stands upon God's score; it therefore
behooves every man so to improve his talents, that
when his Great Master shall call him to reckoning, he
may receive his own with advantage.

Sin and shame ever go together. He that would be
freed from the last must be sure to shun the company
of the first.

God doth many times both reward and punish for one
and the same action; as we see in Jehu, he is
rewarded with a kingdom to the fourth generation for
taking vengeance on the house of Ahab and yet a
little while (sath God) and I will avenge the blood
of Jezerel upon the house of Jehu; he was rewarded
for the matter and yet punished for the manner, which
should warn him that doth any special service for God
to fix his eye on the command, and not on his own

ends, lest he meet with Jehu's reward which will end
in punishment.*

60

He that would be content with a mean condition must
not cast his eye upon one that is in a far better
estate than himself, but let him look upon him that
is lower than he is, and if he sees, that such a one
bears poverty comfortably, it will help to quiet him
but if that will not do, let him look on his own
unworthiness, and that will make him say with Jacob,
I am less than the least of thy mercies.

61

Corn is produced with much labour (as the husbandman
well knows) and some land asks much more pains than
some other doth to be brought into tilth, yet all
must be plowed and harrowed. Some children (like
sour land) are of so tough and morose a dispo[si]tion
that the plough of correction must make long furrows
on their back and the harrow of discipline go often
over them, before they be fit soil to sow the seed of
morality, much less of grace in them. But when by
prudent nurture they are brought into a fit capacity,
let the seed of good instruction and exhortation be
sown in the spring of their youth, and a plentiful
crop may be expected in the harvest of their years.

62

As man is called the little world, so his heart may
be called the little commonwealth; his more fixed and
resolved thoughts are like to inhabitants, his slight
and flitting thoughts are like passengers that travel
to and fro continually. Here is also the great court
of justice erected, which is alway kept by
conscience, who is both accuser, excuser, witness,
and judge, whom no bribes can pervert, nor flattery
cause to favour but as he finds the evidence, so he
absolves or condemns; yea, so absolute is this court
of judicature that there is no appeal from it. No,
not to the court of heaven itself, for if our
conscience and condemns us, he also who is greater
far than our conscience will do it much more; but he
that would have boldness to go to the throne of grace
to be accepted there must be sure to carry a

77

certificate from the court of conscience that he stands right there.

63

He that would keep a pure heart and lead a blameless life must let himself alway in the aweful presence of God; the consideration of his all seeing eye will be a bridle to restrain from evil and a spur to quicken on to good duties; we certainly dream of some remoteness betwixt God and us or else we should not so often fail in our whole course of life as we do, but he that with David sets the Lord alway in sight will not sin against him.

64

We see in orchards, some trees so fruitful that the weight of their burden is the breaking of their limbs, some again are but meanly loaden, and some have nothing to show but leaves only, and some among them are dry stocks. So is it in the church, which is God's orchard: there are some eminent Christians that are so frequent in good duties, that many times, the weight thereof impares both their bodies and estates, and there are some (and they are sincere ones too) who have not attained to that fruitfulness, although they aim at perfection. And again there are others that have nothing to commend them but only a gay profession, and these are but leavie Christians which are in as much danger of being cut down as the dry stock, for both cumber the ground.

65

We see in the firmament there is but one sun among the multitude of stars and those stars also, to differ much one from the other, in regard of bigness and brightness, yet all receive their light from that one sun; so is it in the church both militant and triumphant, there is but one Christ, who is the Sun of righteousness, in the midst of an innumerable company of saints and angels. Those saints have their degrees even in this life: some are stars of the first magnitude, and some of a less degree, and others (and they indeed the most in number) but small and obscure; yet all receive their luster (be it more or less) from the glorious Sun that enlightens all in all, and if some of them shine so bright while they move on earth, how transcendently splendid shall they be when they are fixed in their heavenly spheres.

66

Men that have walked very extravagantly and at last bethink themselves of turning to God, the first thing which they eye is how to reform their ways rather than to beg forgiveness for their sins; nature looks more at a compensation than at a pardon, but he that will not come for mercy without money and without price but bring his filthy rags to barter for it shall meet with miserable disappointment, going away empty, bearing the reproach of his pride and folly.

67

All the works and doings of God are wonderful, but none more awful than his great work of election and reprobation; when we consider how many good parents have had bad children, and again how many bad parents have had pious children, it should make us adore the Sovereinty of God, who will not be tied to time nor place, nor yet to persons, but takes and chooses, when and where and whom he pleases. It should also teach the children of godly parents to walk with fear and trembling, lest they, through unbelief, fall short of a promise; it may also be a support to such as have or had wicked parents, that if they abide not in unbelief, God is able to graff* them in, the upshot of all should make us with the Apostle to admire the justice and mercy of God and say how unsearchable are his ways and his footsteps past finding out.

68

The gifts that God bestows on the sons of men are not only abused but most commonly employed for a clean contrary end than that which they were given for, as health, wealth and honour, which might be so many steps to draw men to God in consideration of his bounty towards them but have driven them the further from him, that they are ready to say: we are lords, we will come no more at thee. If outward blessings be not as wings to help us mount upwards, they will

certainly prove clogs and weights that will pull us
lower downward.

69

All the comforts of this life may be compared to the
gourd of Jonah, that notwithstanding we take great
delight for a season in them and find their shadow
very comfortable; yet there is some worm or other, of
discontent, of fear, or grief that lies at the root,
which in great part withers the pleasure which else
we should take in them, and well it is that we
perceive a decay in their greenness, for were earthly
comforts permanent, who would look for heavenly?

70

All men are truly said to be tenants at will, and it
may as truly be said that all have a lease of their
lives, some longer, some shorter, as it pleases our
Great Landlord to let. All have their bounds set
over which they cannot pass, and till the expiration
of that time, no dangers, no sickness, no pains nor
troubles, shall put a period to our days. The
certainty that that time will come, together, with
the uncertainty, how, where, and when, should make us
so to number our days as to apply our hearts to
wisdom, that when we are put out of these houses of
clay, we may be sure of an everlasting habitation
that fades not away.

71

All weak and diseased bodies have hourly momentos of
their immortality. But the soundest of men have
likewise their nightly monitor, but the emblem of
death, which is their sleep (for so is death often
called) and not only their death, but their grave is
lively represented before their eyes by beholding
their bed; the morning may remind them of the
resurrection, and the Sun approaching, of the
appearing of the Sun of righteousness, at whose
coming they shall all arise out of their beds; the
long night shall fly away, and the day of eternity
shall never end. Seeing these things must be, what
manner of persons ought we to be, in all good
conversation?

72

As the brands of a fire, if once severed, will of
themselves go out, although you use no other means to
extinguish them, so distance of place together with
length of time (if there be no intercourse) will cool
the affections of intimate friends, though there
should be no displeasence between them.

73

A good name is as a precious ointment, and it is a
great favour to have a good repute among good men;
yet it is not that which commends us to God, for by
his balance we must be weighed, and by his judgement
we must be tried, and as he passes the sentence, so
shall we stand.

74

Well doth the Apostle call riches deceitful riches,
and they may truly be compared to deceitful friends
who speak fair and promise much but perform nothing,
and so leave those in the lurch that most relied on
them; so is it with wealth, honours and pleasures of
this world which miserably delude men and make them
put great confidence in them, but when death
threatens and distress lays hold upon them, they
prove like the reeds of Egypt that pierce instead of
supporting,* like empty wells in the time of drought,
that those that go to find water in them, return with
their empty pitchers ashamed.

75

It is admirable to consider the power of faith, but
which all things are (almost) possible to be done; it
can remove mountains (if need were), it hath stayed
the course of the sun, raised the dead, cast out
devils, reversed the order of nature, quenched the
violence of fire, made the water become firm footing
for Peter to walk on; nay more than all these, it
hath overcome the Omnipotent himself, as when Moses
intercedes for the people, God sath* to him, let me
alone that I may destroy them; as if Moses had been
able by the hand of faith to hold the ever lasting
arms of the mighty God of Jacob, yea Jacob himself
when he wrestled with God face to face in Penuel.

Let me go, sath that Angel. I will not let thee go,
replies Jacob, till thou bless me. Faith is not only
thus potent but it is so necessary that without faith
there is no salvation; therefore with all our
seekings and gettings, let us above all seek to
obtain this pearl of prize.

76

Some Christians do by their lusts and corruptions as
the Isralites did by the Canaanites, not destroy them
but put them under tribute, for that they could do
(as they thought) with less hazard and more profit,
but what was the issue? They became a snare unto
them, pricks in their eyes and horns in their sides,
and at last overcame them and kept them under
slavery; so it is most certain that those that are
disobedient to the command of God and endeavor not to
the utmost to drive out all their accursed inmates,
but make a league with them, they shall at last fall
into perpetual bondage under them unless the great
deliverer, Christ Jesus, come to their rescue.

77

God hath by his providence so ordered that no one
country hath all commodities with it self, but what
it wants another shall supply, that so there may be a
mutual commerce through the world. As it is with
countries so it is with men; there was never yet any
one man that had all excellences. Let his parts
natural and acquired, spiritual and moral, be never
so large, yet he stands in need of something which
another man hath (perhaps meaner than himself) which
shows us perfection is not below, as also that God
will have us beholden one to another.

My honoured and dear Mother intended to have filled
up this book with the like observations but was
prevented by death. (This note written by Anne
Bradstreet's son, Simon.)

*Please refer to "Notes."

82

HERE FOLLOWS SOME VERSES UPON THE BURNING OF MY HOUSE, JULY 10, 1666

COPIED OUT OF A LOOSE PAPER

In silent night when rest I took
For sorrow near I did not look,
I wakened was with thund'ring noise
And piteous shreiks of dreadful voice;
That fearful sound of fire and fire,
Let no man know is my desire.
I starting up the light did spy,
And to my God my heart did cry
To strengthen me in my distress
And not to leave me succourless;
Then coming out beheld a space
The flame consume my dwelling place;
And when I could not longer look
I blest his Name that gave and took,
That laid my goods now in the dust,
Yea so it was, and so 'twas just;
It was his own, it was not mine;
Far be it that I should repine;
He might of all justly bereft,
And yet sufficient for us left;
When by the ruins oft I passed
My sorrowing eyes aside did cast
And here and there the places spy
Where oft I sat and long did lie:
Here stood that trunk, there that chest,
There lay that store I counted best;
My pleasant things in ashes lie,
And them behold no more shall I;
Under thy roof no guest shall sit,
Nor at thy table eat a bit;
No pleasant tale shall e'er be told
Nor things recounted done of old;
No candle e'er shall shine in thee
Nor bridegroom's voice e'er heard shall be;
In silence ever shalt thou lie,
Adieu, Adieu; all's vanity;
Then straight I 'gin my heart to chide
And did thy wealth on earth abide?
Didst fix thy hope on mould'ring dust,
The arm of flesh didst make thy trust?

Raise up thy thoughts above the sky
That dunghill mists away may fly.
Thou hast a house on high erect
Framed by that almighty Architect,
With glory richly furnishèd,
Stands permanent though this be fled;
It's purchased and paid for too
By him who hath enough to do;
A prize so vast as is unknown
Yet by his gift is made thine own;
There's wealth enough I need no more,
Farewell my pelf,* farewell my store;
The world no longer let me love,
My hope and treasure lies above.

*pelf: riches.

AS WEARY PILGRIM NOW AT REST

As weary pilgrim, now at rest,
  Hugs with delight his silent nest,
His wasted limbs, now lie full soft
  That mirey steps have trodden oft,
Blesses himself, to think upon
  His dangers past, and travailes done;
The burning sun no more shall heat,
  Nor stormy rains, on him shall beat;
The briars and thorns no more shall scratch
  Nor hungry wolves at him shall catch;
He erring paths no more shall tread
  Nor wild fruits eat, instead of bread,
For waters cold he doth not long
  For thirst no more shall parch his tongue;
No rugged stones his feet shall gaule
  Nor stumps nor rocks cause him to fall;
All cares and fears, he bids farewell
  And means in safety now to dwell;
A pilgrim I, on earth, perplexed
  With sins, with cares, and sorrows vexed
By age and pains brought to decay,
  And my clay house mould'ring away;
Oh how I long to be at rest
  And soar on high among the blest,
This body shall in silence sleep
  Mine eyes no more shall ever weep,
No fainting fits shall me assail
  Nor grinding pains my body frail
With cares and fears ne'er cumbered be
  Nor losses know, nor sorrows see;
What though my flesh shall there consume
  It is the bed Christ did perfume
And when a few years shall be gone
  This mortal shall be clothed upon;
A corrupt carcass down it lies
  A glorious body it shall rise;
In weakness and dishonour sown
  In power 'tis raised by Christ alone;
Then soul and body shall unite
  And of their Maker have the sight;

Such lasting joys shall there behold
    As ear ne'er heard nor tongue e'er told;
Lord make me ready for that day,
    Then come, dear Bridegroom, come away.

August 31, 1669

EXTANT COPIES, NOTES, AND BIBLIOGRAPHY

Location of Extant Copies of Copy Texts:
Several Poems. . .Boston: John Foster, 1678,
and the Andover Manuscript.

Copies of Several Poems are in these libraries:
American Antiquarian Society, Worcester,
Massachusetts; Beinecke Library, Yale University, two
copies with errata leaves; Boston Public Library, two
copies (the Prince copy with errata leaf); British
Museum; Brown University, Harris collection; Henry E.
Huntington Library; Houghton Library, Harvard
University, two copies; John Carter Brown Library,
Brown University; Library of Congress; Massachusetts
Historical Society; New York Public Library; Stephens
Memorial Library, North Andover, Massachusetts. A
private copy is owned by Miss Elizabeth Wade White,
Middlebury, Connecticut and another is in an
anonymous private library, Boston, Massachusetts.

The only extant manuscript called the "Andover
Manuscript" is now conserved at the Houghton Library,
Harvard University. "Meditations Divine and Morall"
appear in Anne Bradstreet's own handwriting. The
remaining poems, letters, and religious experiences
were copied by the poet's son Simon from an original
no longer believed to be in existence. John Harvard
Ellis used this manuscript in preparing his edition
of Bradstreet's work.

Sarah Bradstreet's signature appears on the fly leaf
and it is believed she was the probable owner of the
manuscript.

Notes

"Contemplations"
Section 33, line 7. Revelations, 2:17.

✓"The Flesh and the Spirit"
lines 86 ff. "The City where I hope to dwell."
Revelations, 21: 10-27 and 22: 1-5.

"The Vanity of All Worldly Things"
lines 1-3. Ecclesiastes, 25.

✓"In Reference to My Children, June 23, 1656.

This date is wrong. Ellis suggested 1658 as appro-
priate. In 1678 editions, date corrected to 1659.
Anne Bradstreet's children introduced as follows:

lines 7-10. Samuel sailed to England on November 6,
1657 and returned home on July 17, 1661.

lines 13-20. Dorothy married the Rev. Seaborn Cotton
of Ipswich, John Cotton's eldest son, on June 25,
1654.

lines 21-26. Sarah married Richard Hubbard of
Ipswich, the brother of historian William Hubbard.

lines 27-32. Simon Bradstreet entered Harvard on
June 25, 1656 and graduated in 1660.

line 33. .."And as his ways increase in strength..."
refers to the fifth child. This must be a misprint
as the fifth child was Hannah. The next male born
was the seventh child, Dudley.

Hannah married Andrew Wiggin of Exeter, New
Hampshire, on June 14, 1659.

Mercy married Major Nathaniel Ward of Medford on
October 31, 1672.

Dudley represented the General Court at Andover and held many important municipal offices later in his life.

John married Sarah Perkins of Topsfield, the daughter of Rev. William Perkins, on June 11, 1677. (Hannah, Mercy and John were still at home when Bradstreet wrote this poem.)

"In Memory of my Daughter in Law, Mrs. Mercy Bradstreet"

The date of this poem, September 6, 1669, is incorrect. Mercy, Samuel's wife, died after the premature birth of another child, Anne, born September 3, 1670. Ellis suggested the date was a misprint for 1670. See Ellis, p. 407 and New England Historical General Register, IX, p. 113 ++.

line 27. Mercy, the one remaining child of five born to Samuel and Mercy, received an education and care at the expense of her grandparents, Simon and Anne Bradstreet. Her birthdate was November 20, 1667. Suffolk Probate Records, Lib. xi, Folder 277278. See Also Ellis, p. 408.

"On My Son's Return Out of England, July 17, 1661"

Samuel, Anne Bradstreet's oldest son, sailed to England in 1657.

line 8. Two ships made the journey. Samuel's arrived in England; the other ship, referred to as Master James Garret's, was lost at sea. All passengers perished. See Gookin, "Historical Collections," 62-63.

line 19. Henry, Duke of Gloucester, and Mary, Princess of Orange, both died of small pox in 1660. There were the brother and sister of Charles II.

line 25. Exodus 19:4.

"Meditations Divine and Moral"

Section 42.   Psalm 119:96.
Section 46.   sath: variant of saith.
               Eccliastes 12:11.

Section 51.   Proverbs 30:15.
Section 55.   Luke 17:15.
Section 56.   sath: variant of saith.
Section 59.   2 Kings 10:30.
Section 67.   graff: variant of graft.
Section 74.   2 Kings 18:21.
Section 75.   sath: variant of saith.

Works by Anne Bradstreet

Bradstreet, Anne. _The Tenth Muse Lately Sprung up in America or Several Poems Compiled with Great Variety of Wit and Learning, Full of Delight._ . London: Bowtell, 1650.

This work is the first literary volume published by a woman from the Massachusetts Bay Colony and what later became America. The forward, written by the poet's brother-in-law, John Woodbridge, acknowledges the poet's talent. Bradstreet's early selections are of a historical, personal, and religious nature.

Bradstreet, Anne. _Several Poems Compiled with Great Variety of Wit and Learning, Full of Delight._ . Boston: John Foster, 1678.

This second edition of Bradstreet's work includes all first edition material as well as several poems and meditations found among her papers after her death. The poet did correct some of the mis-spellings and errors found in the first edition.

Bradstreet, Anne. _Several Poems Compiled with Great Variety of Wit and Learning, Full of Delight._ . Boston: no publisher given, 1758.

This third edition of Bradstreet's work has many changes in the text. Generally, this edition is not considered a major resource. Neither the poet nor a reputable editor worked on this edition.

Bradstreet, Anne Dudley. _The Works of Anne Bradstreet in Prose and Verse._ ed. John Harvard Ellis. Charlestown, Mass.: Abram E. Cutter, 1867.

This work reprints the entire contents of the Bradstreet first edition. In addition, it includes what came to be known as the "Andover Manuscript," a series of works left by the poet to her family.

Bradstreet, Anne. The Poems of Mrs. Anne Bradstreet
(1612-1672). Together with Her Prose Remains
with an Introduction by Charles Eliot Norton.
New York: The Duodecimos, 1897.

Norton crtiticizes Ellis's edition somewhat
unmercifully. Although he mentions Ellis's
defects, he does have his own. Among them is
the notion that Anne Bradstreet was a "minor"
writer and concerned with domestic or
unimportant topics as subjects for her works.

Bradstreet, Anne. The Works of Anne Bradstreet in
Prose and Verse. ed. John Harvard Ellis.
Gloucester, Massachusetts: Peter Smith, 1932
and 1962.

These are reprints of Ellis's 1867 edition.

Bradstreet, Anne. The Tenth Muse (1650) and, From
the Manuscripts, Meditations Divine and Moral
Together with Letters and Occasional Pieces. . .
ed. Josephine K. Piercy. Gainesville, Florida:
Scholars' Facsimiles and Reprints, 1965.

Piercy's introductory remarks focus on Anne
Bradstreet's childhood and, to some extent, her
work. The major problem with the reproduction
is its unevenness and, therefore, its limited
value because of technical reproduction quality.

Bradstreet, Anne. The Works of Anne Bradstreet. ed.
Jeannine Hensley. Cambridge, Massachusetts:
Belknap Press, 1967.

This is a useful edition although the editing
techniques take some liberties with the original
material. An introduction by poet Adrienne Rich
is valuable in understanding Anne Bradstreet as
a woman and as an artist.

Bradstreet, Anne. The Poems of Anne Bradstreet. ed.
Robert Hutchinson. New York: Dover, 1969.

Hutchinson's introduction provides the
standard Bradstreet information, but he does
present his view sympathetically. Selected
poems are included.

Bradstreet, Anne. <u>The Complete Works</u>. eds. Joseph
    McElrath, Jr. and Allen F. Robb. Boston:
    Twayne, 1981.

    This ambitious work falls short in two areas;
first, the selection of the first edition with
its many errors as copy text; and secondly, its
rather simplistic concept that Bradstreet really
faced only minimal barriers in terms of her
artistic development and acceptance.

Manuscripts

The Andover Manuscript. Houghton Library, Harvard
    University Library, Cambridge, Massachusetts.

    This manuscript, the only material in the
poet's own hand to survive, was for years stored
at the Stevens Memorial Library at Andover,
Massachusetts which still houses a collection of
works about the poet. For conservation
purposes, the manuscript is now kept at the
Houghton Library. "Meditations Divine and
Moral" is in the poet's hand; "Religious
Experiences and Occasional Pieces" is copied
from another notebook. This copy is in the hand
of the poet's son Simon.

Works on Anne Bradstreet

Bailey, Sarah L. *Historical Sketches of Andover Massachusetts.* Boston: Houghton Mifflin, 1880.

This work provides information about important figures in the history of Andover, Massachusetts. One chapter is devoted to Anne Bradstreet and her works. Although some of the information is now dated, the chapter is still valuable for its information about the poet's life in early Andover's settlement.

Berryman, John. *Homage to Mistress Bradstreet.* New York: Farrar, Straus, 1956.

Poet Berryman praises Anne Bradstreet's artistic achievements as well as her courageous acts as a Christian mother.

Butts, Miriam. *Anne Bradstreet: The Easterling.* Unpublished paper. North Andover, Massachusetts: Stevens Memorial Library, April 1979.

This paper highlights the time Anne Bradstreet spent in England as a young girl. Also emphasized is the importance of needlework and "womanly arts" in the seventeenth century.

Caldwell, Colonel Luther. *An Account of Anne Bradstreet, the Puritan Poetess and Kindred Topics.* Boston: Damrell and Upham, 1898.

Caldwell's insightful remarks about Bradstreet's contribution as a New England artist and a unique literary figure are valuable resources.

Campbell, Helen. *Anne Bradstreet and Her Time.* Tampa, Florida: Russell, 1891.

This full-length work focuses primarily on the historical period and traces common beliefs and attitudes toward seventeenth century women. Some explication of Bradstreet's prose and poetry is included.

Cummings, Abbott Lowell. "Not Anne Bradstreet House," *Boston Herald*, October 28, 1956.

This article establishes that the house long recognized as Anne Bradstreet's Andover house was, in fact, not.

Duyckinck, Evert A., and George L. *Cyclopaedia of American Literature*. New York: C. Scribner, 1855. I, 47-52.

This review presents a negative perspective. Bradstreet is attacked as someone with a "lack of taste" and "imagination." The material is biased and quite sexist by modern standards.

Fuess, Claude M. "Andover's Anne Bradstreet, Puritan Poet," *Andover Symbol of New England*. Andover: Andover Historical Society, 1959.

This is one of several articles published by the Historical Society which shows how Anne Bradstreet's works were symbols of early Andover life and the New England culture of her time.

Hamblen, Abigail A. "Anne Bradstreet: Portrait of a Puritan Lady," *Cresset*. 32, i (1968), 11-13.

This article proposes that Anne Bradstreet was really a conformist and not a feminist.

Hensley, Jeannine. "The Editor of Anne Bradstreet's *Several Poems*." *American Literature*. 35 (1964), 502-504.

Hensley documents evidence suggesting John Rogers' editing 1678 Bradstreet edition. She cites Rogers' poem and discovery of an errata page as clear indicators. Rogers was President of Harvard College and an admirer of Bradstreet's work.

Jantz, Harold S. "First Century of New England Verse." *American Antiquarian Society Proceedings*, 53 (October 1943), 252-254.

A critical view of Bradstreet's work that is
hampered only by its emphasis on the earlier Du
Bartas period.

Jantz, Harold S. The First Century of New England
    Verse. New York: Russell and Russell, 1962.
    36-38, 183.

The author provides evidence of Bradstreet's
charm and real talent as a poet.

McCallum, Jane Y. Women Pioneers. Richmond, New
    York, 1929.

A chapter on Anne Bradstreet's early
struggles is included.

Makin, Bathsua. An Essay to Revive the Ancient
    Education of Gentlewomen in Religion, Manners,
    Arts & Tongues. London: Thomas Parkhurst,
    1673.

This essay, like many of its time, makes
pleasant note of appreciation for Bradstreet's
work, thus showing her work was noted in
England.

Mather, Cotton. Magnalia Christi Americana. London:
    Printed for Thomas Parkhurst, 1702. Book 2.
    Reprinted at Hartford: Roberts & Burry
    Printers, 1820. 133-135.

A typical review of Thomas Dudley's life in
England is followed by the often quoted praise
of Dudley's daughter as a star in her father's
crown. Beyond Mather's obvious verbosity and
occasional overstatement, one finds valuable
information about this period and the important
people who lived in it.

Morison, Samuel Eliot. "Mistress Anne Bradstreet,"
    Builders of the Bay Colony. Boston: Houghton
    Mifflin Riverside Press, 1930.

Morison criticizes previously biased
criticism of Bradstreet's work and urges she
receive credit for her moral qualities and her

101

artistic contributions. This is an excellent source.

Morison, Samuel Eliot. The Intellectual Life of Colonial New England. New York: New York University Press, 1956.

Excellent sources for its information on Anne Bradstreet and its general discussion of printing practices among American clergy and political figures.

Pearson, Charles William. "Early American Poetry." Literary and Biographical Essays. Boston: 1908. 16-21.

Pearson acknowledges Bradstreet as a "genuine poet" and indicates she may receive more praise in the future than she had in the past. This article represents one of the first evenhanded criticisms of Bradstreet's work.

Phillips, Edward. "Women among the Moderns Eminent for Poetry," Theatrum Poetarum. London: Printed Charles Smith, 1675.

Since Phillips was Milton's nephew, this article, although briefly mentioning Anne Bradstreet as a poet, is often cited.

Piercy, Josephine K. Anne Bradstreet. New Haven: College and University Press, 1965.

Piercy's work covers Bradstreet's historical and literary development. Extensive attempts are made to identify classical sources for Bradstreet's works. Bibliography included.

Richardson, Lyon N. "Anne Bradstreet." Dictionary of American Biography. 1. New York: C. Scribner, 1928.

This article provides some facts about Bradstreet's life, but the assessment of her work is not favorable.

Spiller, Robert E. et. al. Literary History of the
United States. New York: Macmillan, 1974.

Spiller's discussion of Anne Bradstreet's
work is generally sexist and ignores the
philosophical and religious beliefs of the
poet's time.

Stanford, Ann. "Anne Bradstreet: An Annotated
Checklist." Early American Literature. 3
(1968-1969). 217-228.

Checklist includes manuscripts, books,
pamphlets, and commentaries about Bradstreet.

Stanford, Ann. "Anne Bradstreet: An Annotated
Checklist." Bulletin of Bibliography. 27
(April-June 1970). 34-37.

A brief checklist of works, articles, and
commentaries.

Stanford, Ann. "Anne Bradstreet as a Meditative
Writer." California English Journal. 2
(Winter, 1966). 24-31.

Stanford describes Bradstreet's use of
meditative and emblematic poetry, especially as
found in the poet's "Contemplations."

Stanford, Ann. "Anne Bradstreet: Dogmatist and
Rebel." New England Quarterly. 39 (1966). 373-
389.

Stanford discusses Bradstreet's desire to
accept Puritan dogma and her own innate doubts
about such beliefs.

Stanford, Ann. Anne Bradstreet: The Worldly
Puritan, An Introduction to Her Poetry. New
York: Burt Franklin, 1975.

Stanford's analysis of Bradstreet's poetic
development and the sources the poet was
familiar with are valuable tools for study.

Stanford, Ann. The Poetry of Anne Bradstreet.
Dissertation. Los Angeles: The University of
California, 1962.

   A careful analysis of Anne Bradstreet's
poetic style and content.

Starrett, Vincent. "The First American Poet."
Freeman. 5 (May 17, 1922). 224-225.

   A sexist and demeaning attitude characterizes
this article.

The Founding of a Nation. ed. Kenneth Silverman.
New York: Collier-Macmillan, 1971.

   This volume contains introductory material
and literature from America's earliest English
period. The Bradstreet material is sexist, but
the editor suggests inclusion of some of her
poems in this anthology.

Trent, William P. et. al. The Cambridge History of
American Literature. 1. New York: Putnam,
1917. 154-156.

   Trent writes "Bradstreet was not a poet; she
was a winsome personality in an unlovely age."

Tyler, Moses Coit. A History of American Literature
During the Colonial Period. 1. New York: G.P.
Putnam, 1897. 277-292.

   Although Tyler criticizes Bradstreet's early
work, he does find merit in her later personal
reflections such as "Contemplations."

Vancura, Z. "Baroque Prose in America." Studies in
English. 4. Prague: Charles University, 1935.
39-88.

   This article illustrates how Bradstreet's
prose meditations reflect stylistic evidence of
the balanced sentence, the neatly turned phrase,
and the apt metaphor.

Warren, Austin. "The Puritan Poets." New England Saints. Ann Arbor: University of Michigan, 1956. 714.

Brief comment on a few Bradstreet poems is followed by comment that the poet is not imitative of Du Bartas' conceits.

Watts, Emily S. The Poetry of American Women. Austin: University of Texas Press, 1977.

Watts comments briefly on Bradstreet, but includes representative selections from the poet's works.

White, Elizabeth Wade. Anne Bradstreet: the Tenth Muse. New York: Oxford University Press, 1971.

White's study is particularly valuable for its solid historical perspective. In addition, the author does a competent job of analyzing Bradstreet poetry.

White, Elizabeth Wade. "The Tenth Muse--A Tercentenary Appraisal of Anne Bradstreet," The William and Mary Quarterly. 8 (July 1951). 355-377.

White emphasizes Bradstreet's recognition by English contemporaries and names her as the first significant women poet of English in America.

White, Trentwell Mason, and P.W. Lehman. Writers of Colonial New England. Boston: Palmer Company, 1929.

The writers acknowledge Bradstreet's biting wit and crackling epigrams in "The Dialogue of Old England and New."

Whicher, George F., ed. Alas, All's Vanity, or a Leaf from the First American Edition of Several Poems by Anne Bradstreet. Boston: 1678. Reprinted in New York: Spiral Press, 1942.

This work contains a final chapter that praises Bradstreet's work.

Other Background Sources

Andrews, Charles M. Colonial Period of American History. 1. New Haven: Yale University Press, 1934.

   This source contains valuable information about the early formation of the Massachusetts Bay Colony and traces the importance of Anne Bradstreet's father and husband as leaders in the new world.

Beard, Charles and Mary. Growth of Social and Intellectual Development. New York: Doubleday, 1960.

   This volume makes reference to the unique educational opportunities women born to the rising middle-class merchants had. Such women as Anne Bradstreet and Ann Hutchinson were among those.

Fiedelson, Charles, Jr. Symbolism and American Literature. University of Chicago: Phoenix Books, 1953.

   Chapter III deals with American traditions and is valuable for information about Puritan thought in America.

Hawke, David. The Colonial Experience. New York: Bobbs-Merrill, 1966.

   This work deals with aspects of everyday life during the early English settlements.

Holliday, Carl. Woman's Life in Colonial Days. Williamstown, Mass.: Corner House Publishers, 1968.

   Chapters on religious life, household duties, social life, and child rearing are important to understanding a woman's role in early American life. Anne Bradstreet and Anne Hutchinson are mentioned.

Hornstein, Jacqueline. "Comic Vision in Literature of Women Before 1800." Regionalism and the Female Imagination. 3 (1977-1978). 11-19.

Since women artists often found humor their only means of dealing with difficult issues, this article has merit.

Hutchinson, Thomas. The History of the Colony of Massachusetts Bay. Boston: Printed by Thomas and John Fleet, 1764.

Chapter 1 provides a detailed picture of the colony from its first settlement to 1638. This information is particularly useful in providing details of Anne Hutchinson's trial and punishment.

Miller, Perry. "Poetry," The American Puritans, Their Prose and Poetry. New York: Doubleday Anchor, 1956.

Miller's chapter on the early American poets and the Puritan poetic ethic sheds light on the important issue of understanding the place poetry had in the Puritan culture. This is particularly relevant because Bradstreet emulated these values even though they were designed for men.

Morgan, Edmund S. The Puritan Dilemma: The Story of John Winthrop. Boston: Little, Brown and Company, 1958.

This study emphasizes the difficult living conditions in New England and the necessity of a close knit religious community. These ideas bear significantly on the consequences of women's roles, and particularly on Winthrop's repression of original thought and expression.

Murdock, Kenneth B. Literature and Theology in Colonial New England. Cambridge: Harvard University Press, 1949.

Murdock's discussion of the close alliance between literature and theology helps the modern

reader understand Bradstreet's deep concern for
religious and meditative subjects.

Schneider, Herbert W. The Puritan Mind. Ann Arbor:
University of Michigan Press, 1958.

Schneider presents an analysis of the
philosophical ideas that governed Puritan life.

Silverman, Kenneth. Colonian American Poetry. New
York: Hafner Publishing Company, 1968.

Silverman evaluates the form, style, and
content of early American poetry with brief
discussion of Anne Bradstreet's work.

Stewart, Randall. American Literature and Christian
Doctrine. Baton Rouge: Louisiana State
University Press, 1958.

Stewart emphasizes the philosophical
implications of early New England writing.
These implications were deeply religious and
structured and have influenced American
literature and culture.

Wilson, Woodrow. A History of the American People.
1. New York: Harper and Row, 1902.

Includes an excellent discussion on early
Colonial life and the role of outspoken women
such as Anne Bradstreet.

Winthrop, John. Winthrop's Journal: History of New
England. 1 and 2. ed. James Kendall Hosmer.
New York: Charles Scribner's Sons, 1908.

These journals are an invaluable source of
information about the life and times of the
Massachusetts Bay Colony. In particular,
descriptions of women and their behavior add
much light upon the roles they played in
Colonial days.

About the Author.

Adelaide P. Amore, a Connecticut native, teaches American literature and writing. In over twenty years of teaching, Professore Amore saw a growing interest in women writers among her students and felt the need to assess women's contributions so as to enhance their place in American letters. An Anne Bradstreet study was the perfect choice to demonstrate the on-going problems faced by women artists who sought public audiences. Continuing her scholarly study through a Yale-Mellon Visiting Faculty Fellowship, Professor Amore developed a new course in American women writers. In addition, a Connecticut Humanities Grant enabled her to discuss with community members the various characterizations of women in the American short story film series.

Long active in political and community affairs, Amore served as elected Selectwoman in the Town of Madison as well as Vice-Chairwoman of the school board. Currently, she serves as Legislative Action Director for the Connecticut State College American Association of University Professors. Amore is a member of the National Council of Teachers of English and the International Women's Writing Guild.

As the mother of two teen-aged sons, Professor Amore has a deep kinship for the centuries old problems women face in combining their domestic and artistic roles. Through Anne Bradstreet's work modern readers will see a reflection of their own lives.